EAT beautiful

Publications International, Ltd.

Microwave Cooking: Microwave ovens vary in wattage. Use the cooking times as guidelines and check for doneness before adding more time.

WARNING: Food preparation, baking and cooking involve inherent dangers: misuse of electric products, sharp electric tools, boiling water, hot stoves, allergic reactions, foodborne illnesses and the like, pose numerous potential risks. Publications International, Ltd. (PIL) assumes no responsibility or liability for any damages you may experience as a result of following recipes, instructions, tips or advice in this publication.

While we hope this publication helps you find new ways to eat delicious foods, you may not always achieve the results desired due to variations in ingredients, cooking temperatures, typos, errors, omissions, or individual cooking abilities.

Let's get social!

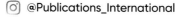 @Publications_International

@PublicationsInternational

www.pilbooks.com

CONTENTS

BREAKFAST

irish porridge with berry compote

MAKES 4 SERVINGS

4 cups plus 1 tablespoon water, divided

½ teaspoon salt

1 cup steel-cut oats

½ teaspoon ground cinnamon

⅓ cup half-and-half

¼ cup packed brown sugar

1 cup fresh strawberries, hulled and quartered

1 container (6 ounces) fresh blackberries

1 container (6 ounces) fresh blueberries

3 tablespoons granulated sugar

1. Bring 4 cups water and salt to a boil in medium saucepan over medium-high heat. Whisk in oats and cinnamon. Reduce heat to medium; simmer, uncovered, 30 to 35 minutes or until water is absorbed and oats are tender. Remove from heat; stir in half-and-half and brown sugar.

2. Meanwhile, combine strawberries, blackberries, blueberries, granulated sugar and remaining 1 tablespoon water in small saucepan; bring to a simmer over medium heat. Cook 8 to 9 minutes or until berries are tender but still hold their shape, stirring occasionally.

3. Divide porridge among four bowls; top with berry compote.

mediterranean frittata

MAKES 4 TO 6 SERVINGS

¼ cup extra virgin olive oil

5 small onions, thinly sliced

1 can (about 14 ounces) whole peeled tomatoes, drained and chopped

4 ounces prosciutto or cooked ham, chopped

¼ cup grated Parmesan cheese

2 tablespoons chopped fresh parsley

½ teaspoon salt

½ teaspoon dried marjoram

¼ teaspoon dried basil

⅛ teaspoon black pepper

6 eggs

2 tablespoons butter

1. Heat oil in large skillet over medium-high heat. Add onions; cook and stir 8 to 10 minutes or until soft and golden. Reduce heat to medium. Add tomatoes; cook 5 minutes. Transfer vegetables to large bowl with slotted spoon; discard drippings. Cool to room temperature.

2. Stir prosciutto, Parmesan, parsley, salt, marjoram, basil and pepper into tomato mixture. Whisk eggs in medium bowl; stir into prosciutto mixture.

3. Preheat broiler. Melt butter in medium broilerproof skillet over medium heat. Reduce heat to low; add egg mixture, spreading evenly. Cook 8 to 10 minutes until all but top ¼ inch of frittata is set; shake pan gently to test. *Do not stir.*

4. Broil frittata about 4 inches from heat 1 to 2 minutes or until top is set. (Do not brown or frittata will be dry.) Cut into wedges. Serve warm or at room temperature.

buckwheat pancakes

MAKES 12 PANCAKES

1 cup buckwheat flour

2 tablespoons cornstarch

2 teaspoons baking powder

¼ teaspoon salt

¼ teaspoon ground cinnamon

1 cup whole milk

1 egg

2 tablespoons butter, melted,
   plus additional for cooking

2 tablespoons maple syrup, plus
   additional for serving

½ teaspoon vanilla

1. Whisk buckwheat flour, cornstarch, baking powder, salt and cinnamon in medium bowl. Whisk milk, egg, 2 tablespoons butter, 2 tablespoons maple syrup and vanilla in small bowl. Gradually whisk into dry ingredients just until combined. Let stand 5 minutes. (Batter will be thick and elastic.)

2. Heat griddle or large nonstick skillet over medium heat. Brush with additional butter. Pour ¼ cupfuls of batter 2 inches apart onto griddle. Cook 2 minutes or until lightly browned and edges begin to bubble. Turn over; cook 2 minutes or until lightly browned. Serve with additional maple syrup.

VARIATION: Add ½ cup blueberries to the batter.

breakfast flats

MAKES 4 SERVINGS

Basic Pizza Dough (recipe
follows)

8 slices bacon, diced

All-purpose flour, for dusting

1½ cups (6 ounces) shredded
medium Cheddar cheese

1 tablespoon olive oil or butter

4 eggs

Coarse salt and black pepper

1. Prepare pizza dough (dough can be made the night before). Preheat oven to 400°F. Line two baking sheets with parchment paper.

2. Heat large nonstick skillet over medium-high heat. Add bacon; cook about 8 minutes or until crisp, stirring occasionally. Drain on paper towel-lined plate.

3. Divide pizza dough into 4 equal portions. Roll out on lightly floured surface into rectangles about 8×4 inches. Place rolled dough onto prepared baking sheets; topping each evenly with cheese and bacon. Bake 10 minutes or until crust is golden brown and crisp and cheese is melted.

4. Heat oil in large nonstick skillet. Fry eggs sunny-side up. Place one egg on each flat; season with salt and pepper. Serve immediately.

basic pizza dough

3 cups all-purpose flour

1 package (¼ ounce) rapid-rise
active dry yeast

1 teaspoon salt

1 cup warm water (120°F)

2 tablespoons olive oil

1. Combine flour, yeast and salt in large bowl of stand mixer. Stir in water and oil to form rough dough. Knead with dough hook at low speed 5 to 7 minutes or until dough is smooth and elastic.

2. Shape dough into a ball. Place in greased bowl; turn to grease top. Cover and let rise in warm place about 45 minutes or until doubled in size. Punch down dough. Shape into a ball; wrap in plastic wrap and refrigerate until ready to use.

maple pecan granola

MAKES ABOUT 6 CUPS

6 tablespoons vegetable oil

¼ cup maple syrup

¼ cup packed dark brown sugar

1½ teaspoons vanilla

½ teaspoon ground cinnamon

½ teaspoon coarse salt

3 cups old-fashioned oats

1½ cups shredded coconut

¾ cup raw pecans, coarsely chopped

¼ cup ground flax seeds

¼ cup water

Plain yogurt or milk (optional)

1. Preheat oven to 350°F. Line large rimmed baking sheet with parchment paper.

2. Whisk oil, maple syrup, brown sugar, vanilla, cinnamon and salt in large bowl. Stir in oats, coconut, pecans and flax seeds until evenly coated. Stir in water. Spread mixture evenly on prepared baking sheet, pressing into even layer.

3. Bake 30 minutes or until mixture is golden brown and fragrant. Cool completely on baking sheet. Serve with yogurt or milk, if desired. Store leftovers in an airtight container at room temperature 1 month.

NOTE: For chunky granola, do not stir during baking. For loose granola, stir every 10 minutes during baking.

green smoothie bowl

MAKES 2 SERVINGS

1 banana, frozen

2 pears, seeded and cut into chunks

2 cups baby kale

1 avocado, pitted and peeled

1 cup ice

½ cup fresh mint leaves (about 6 sprigs)

4 strawberries, stemmed and sliced

2 tablespoons granola

2 teaspoons chia seeds

2 tablespoons shredded coconut

1. Combine banana, pears, kale, avocado, ice and mint in blender; blend until smooth. Pour into 2 bowls.

2. Arrange strawberries, granola, chia seeds and coconut in lines across smoothies. Serve immediately.

berry buckwheat scones

MAKES 8 SCONES

1¼ cups all-purpose flour

¾ cup buckwheat flour, plus additional for dusting

¼ cup packed brown sugar

1 tablespoon baking powder

½ teaspoon salt

½ cup (1 stick) cold unsalted butter, cut into pieces

¾ cup fresh raspberries

¾ cup fresh blackberries

½ cup whipping cream

1 egg

1 tablespoon granulated sugar

Jam or lemon curd (optional)

1. Preheat oven to 375°F. Line baking sheet with parchment paper.

2. Combine all-purpose flour, ¾ cup buckwheat flour, brown sugar, baking powder and salt in food processor; pulse until combined. Add butter; pulse until pea-sized pieces of butter remain. Transfer mixture to large bowl; stir in berries.

3. Whisk cream and egg in small bowl. Stir cream mixture into flour mixture until soft dough forms.

4. Transfer dough to work surface lightly dusted with buckwheat flour; gently pat into 8-inch round about ¾ inch thick. Cut into 8 equal wedges. Place wedges 1½ inches apart on prepared baking sheet. Sprinkle tops with granulated sugar.

5. Bake 20 to 25 minutes or until golden. Remove to wire rack; cool 10 minutes. Serve warm with jam or lemon curd, if desired.

whole wheat blueberry pancakes

MAKES 12 PANCAKES

½ cup whole wheat pastry flour

½ cup all-purpose flour

1 teaspoon baking powder

½ teaspoon baking soda

⅛ teaspoon salt

1 egg white

1 cup buttermilk

3 tablespoons canola oil, divided

1½ cups fresh blueberries, divided

½ cup maple syrup

1. Whisk both flours, baking powder, baking soda and salt in medium bowl. Whisk egg white in small bowl. Whisk in buttermilk and 1 tablespoon oil. Add to flour mixture; mix just until dry ingredients are moistened. Stir in 1 cup blueberries.

2. Heat 1 tablespoon oil in large nonstick skillet over medium heat. Drop batter by scant ¼ cupfuls into skillet. Cook 2 to 3 minutes or until bottoms are golden brown. Turn; cook 1 to 2 minutes longer or until bottoms are golden brown, adding additional oil as needed. Keep warm in 200°F oven while making remaining pancakes.

3. Combine remaining ½ cup blueberries and maple syrup in microwavable bowl; microwave on HIGH 20 to 30 seconds or until warm. Spoon over pancakes.

spinach, mushroom, egg and gruyère rollups

MAKES 4 SERVINGS

1 tablespoon plus 4 teaspoons olive oil, divided

1 shallot, thinly sliced

1 bag (5 to 6 ounces) fresh baby spinach

1 clove garlic, minced

¾ teaspoon salt, divided

8 ounces cremini mushrooms, thinly sliced

¼ teaspoon black pepper, divided

2 pieces flatbread (about 9×11 inches), lightly toasted

⅔ cup shredded Gruyère or Swiss cheese

6 eggs

2 tablespoons milk

2 teaspoons Dijon mustard

1. Heat 2 teaspoons oil in large nonstick skillet over medium heat. Add shallot; cook and stir 5 to 6 minutes until softened. Increase heat to medium-high. Add spinach; cook 2 minutes or until wilted. Add garlic and ¼ teaspoon salt; cook and stir 1 minute. Transfer to medium bowl.

2. Heat 1 tablespoon oil in same skillet over medium-high heat. Add mushrooms, ¼ teaspoon salt and ⅛ teaspoon pepper; cook 6 minutes until browned, stirring occasionally.

3. Place half of spinach and mushrooms on each flatbread; top with cheese.

4. Whisk eggs in large bowl. Add remaining ¼ teaspoon salt, ⅛ teaspoon pepper, milk and mustard.

5. Heat remaining 2 teaspoons oil in same skillet over medium-high heat. Add egg mixture; cook about 1 minute until eggs are set but not dry, stirring frequently.

6. Place cooked eggs on vegetables; roll up flatbread and cut in half.

quinoa and oat muesli

MAKES ABOUT 7 CUPS

1 cup uncooked quinoa

3 cups old-fashioned rolled oats

¾ cup coarsely chopped almonds

¼ cup shredded coconut

½ teaspoon ground cinnamon

½ cup toasted wheat germ

¼ cup ground flaxseed

1¼ cups dried or freeze-dried fruit

Yogurt, milk or almond milk

1. Preheat oven to 350°F. Spread quinoa in single layer on large rimmed baking sheet. Bake 8 to 10 minutes until toasted and golden brown, stirring frequently. (Quinoa will make a slight popping sound when almost done.) Cool completely. Place in large bowl.

2. Combine oats, almonds, coconut and cinnamon in large bowl. Spread in even layer on baking sheet. Bake 15 minutes or until mixture is toasted and fragrant but not burnt. Cool completely.

3. Add oat mixture, wheat germ, flaxseed and dried fruit to quinoa; mix well. Serve with yogurt or milk.

chorizo-potato hash with crisp crumb topping

MAKES 6 SERVINGS

1 naan or pita breads, torn into uneven pieces

6 tablespoons plus 1 teaspoon olive oil, divided

Salt and black pepper

1 pound Mexican chorizo, casings removed

1 onion, diced

1 yellow bell pepper, diced

1 red bell pepper, diced

2 Russet potatoes, peeled, shredded, rinsed and squeezed dry

1 green onion, sliced diagonally

1. Place naan pieces in food processor; pulse until small crumbs form. Transfer to large bowl; toss with 2 tablespoons oil.

2. Heat large skillet over medium heat. Add crumbs; cook 6 to 8 minutes or until browned and toasted, stirring occasionally. Season with salt and black pepper; transfer to small bowl.

3. Heat 1 teaspoon oil in same skillet over medium-high heat. Add chorizo; cook about 5 minutes or until browned, breaking up sausage with wooden spoon. Transfer to paper towel-lined plate. Heat 1 tablespoon oil in same skillet; add onion and bell peppers; cook 8 minutes or until tender, stirring occasionally. Season with salt and black pepper. Transfer to medium bowl.

4. Heat remaining 3 tablespoons oil in same skillet. Add potatoes in even layer; cook about 3 minutes or until browned and beginning to crisp on bottom. Turn potatoes, continue to cook about 10 minutes or until tender and evenly browned, stirring occasionally. Season with salt and black pepper. Stir in chorizo and vegetable mixture; cook 2 minutes until heated through. Top with bread crumbs and green onion.

SALADS

colorful coleslaw

MAKES 4 TO 6 SERVINGS

¼ **head green cabbage, shredded or thinly sliced**

¼ **head red cabbage, shredded or thinly sliced**

1 **small yellow or orange bell pepper, thinly sliced**

1 **small jicama, peeled and julienned**

¼ **cup thinly sliced green onions**

2 **tablespoons chopped fresh cilantro**

¼ **cup vegetable oil**

¼ **cup fresh lime juice**

1 **teaspoon salt**

⅛ **teaspoon black pepper**

1. Combine cabbage, bell pepper, jicama, green onions and cilantro in large bowl.

2. Whisk oil, lime juice, salt and black pepper in small bowl until well blended. Pour over vegetables; toss to coat. Cover and refrigerate 2 to 6 hours for flavors to blend.

NOTE: This coleslaw makes a great topping for tacos and sandwiches.

chicken waldorf salad

MAKES 4 SERVINGS

DRESSING

- ⅓ cup balsamic vinegar
- 2 tablespoons Dijon mustard
- 2 teaspoons minced garlic
- ½ teaspoon salt
- ¼ teaspoon black pepper
- ⅔ cup extra virgin olive oil

SALAD

- 8 cups mixed greens
- 1 large Granny Smith apple, cut into ½-inch pieces
- ⅔ cup diced celery
- ⅔ cup halved red seedless grapes
- 12 to 16 ounces sliced grilled chicken breasts
- ½ cup candied walnuts or toasted walnuts
- ½ cup crumbled blue cheese

1. For dressing, combine vinegar, mustard, garlic, salt and pepper in medium bowl; mix well. Gradually whisk in oil in thin steady stream until well blended.

2. For salad, combine mixed greens, apple, celery and grapes in large bowl. Add half of dressing; toss to coat. Top with chicken, walnuts and cheese; drizzle with additional dressing.

heirloom tomato quinoa salad

MAKES 4 SERVINGS

1 cup uncooked quinoa

2 cups water

2 tablespoons extra virgin olive oil

1 tablespoon lemon juice

1 clove garlic, minced

½ teaspoon salt

2 cups assorted heirloom grape tomatoes (red, yellow or a combination), halved

¼ cup crumbled feta cheese

¼ cup chopped fresh basil

1. Place quinoa in fine-mesh strainer; rinse well under cold running water. Combine quinoa and 2 cups water in small saucepan; bring to a boil. Reduce heat to low; cover and simmer 10 to 15 minutes or until quinoa is tender and water is absorbed.

2. Meanwhile, whisk oil, lemon juice, garlic and salt in large bowl until well blended. Gently stir in tomatoes and quinoa. Cover and refrigerate at least 30 minutes.

3. Stir in cheese just before serving. Top each serving with basil.

house salad

MAKES 4 SERVINGS

DRESSING

- ½ cup mayonnaise
- ½ cup white wine vinegar
- ¼ cup grated Parmesan cheese
- 1 tablespoon extra virgin olive oil
- 1 tablespoon lemon juice
- 1 tablespoon sugar
- 1 clove garlic, minced
- ¾ teaspoon Italian seasoning
- ½ teaspoon salt
- ½ teaspoon black pepper

SALAD

- 1 package (10 ounces) Italian salad blend
- 2 plum tomatoes, thinly sliced
- 1 cup croutons
- ½ cup thinly sliced red or green bell pepper
- ½ cup thinly sliced red onion
- ¼ cup sliced black olives
- Pepperoncini (optional)

1. For dressing, whisk mayonnaise, vinegar, cheese, oil, lemon juice, sugar, garlic, Italian seasoning, salt and black pepper in medium bowl until well blended and sugar is dissolved.

2. For salad, place lettuce in large bowl; top with tomatoes, croutons, bell pepper, onion, olives and pepperoncini, if desired. Add dressing; toss to coat.

rainbow taco salad

MAKES 4 SERVINGS

DRESSING

- ¼ **cup mayonnaise**
- ¼ **cup plain yogurt or sour cream**
- 1 **tablespoon lime juice**
- ½ **teaspoon chipotle chili powder**
- 1 **clove garlic, minced**
- ¼ **cup crumbled cotija or feta cheese or grated Parmesan cheese**
- ¼ **cup chopped fresh cilantro**

SALAD

- 2 **cups finely shredded red and/ or green cabbage**
- 2 **avocados, thinly sliced**
- 2 **cups quartered cherry tomatoes**
- 1 **cup cooked black beans**
- 1 **seedless cucumber, thinly sliced**

  Assorted sliced radishes (optional)

  Optional toppings: black and white sesame seeds, pomegranate seeds and fresh herbs such as cilantro, parsley and/or basil

1. For dressing, whisk mayonnaise, yogurt, lime juice, chili powder and garlic in small bowl. Stir in cheese and cilantro. Thin with water to desired drizzling consistency, if needed.

2. For salad, arrange cabbage, avocados, tomatoes, beans and cucumber in four bowls. Top with radishes and desired toppings. Drizzle dressing over salad.

zesty zucchini chickpea salad

MAKES 4 TO 6 SERVINGS

3 medium zucchini (about 6 ounces each)

½ teaspoon salt

5 tablespoons white vinegar

1 clove garlic, minced

¼ teaspoon dried thyme

½ cup extra virgin olive oil

1 cup cooked chickpeas

½ cup sliced pitted black olives

3 green onions, minced

1 canned chipotle pepper in adobo sauce, drained, seeded, minced

1 ripe avocado, cut into ½-inch cubes

⅓ cup crumbled feta cheese

Boston lettuce leaves and sliced tomatoes (optional)

1. Cut zucchini lengthwise into halves; cut halves crosswise into ¼-inch-thick slices. Place in medium bowl; sprinkle with salt. Toss to mix. Spread zucchini on several layers of paper towels. Let stand at room temperature 30 minutes to drain.

2. Combine vinegar, garlic and thyme in large bowl. Gradually whisk in oil in thin steady stream until well blended.

3. Pat zucchini dry; add to dressing. Add chickpeas, olives and green onions; toss to coat. Cover and refrigerate at least 30 minutes or up to 4 hours, stirring occasionally.

4. Add chipotle pepper to salad just before serving. Add avocado and cheese; toss to mix.

5. If desired, line shallow bowls or small plates with lettuce and tomato slices. Top with salad.

strawberry poppy seed chicken salad

MAKES 4 SERVINGS

DRESSING

- ¼ **cup white wine vinegar**
- 2 **tablespoons orange juice**
- 1 **tablespoon sugar**
- 2 **teaspoons poppy seeds**
- 1½ **teaspoons Dijon mustard**
- ½ **teaspoon salt**
- ½ **teaspoon minced dried onion**
- ½ **cup vegetable oil**

SALAD

- 8 **cups romaine lettuce**
- 1 **package (12 to 16 ounces) grilled or roasted chicken breast strips**
- ¾ **cup fresh pineapple chunks**
- ¾ **cup sliced fresh strawberries**
- ¾ **cup fresh blueberries**
- 1 **navel orange, peeled and sectioned**
- ¼ **cup chopped toasted pecans**

1. For dressing, combine vinegar, orange juice, sugar, poppy seeds, mustard, salt and dried onion in small bowl; mix well. Gradually whisk in oil in thin steady stream until well blended.

2. For salad, combine romaine and two thirds of dressing in large bowl; toss gently to coat. Divide salad among four plates; top with chicken, pineapple, strawberries, blueberries, oranges and pecans. Serve with remaining dressing.

fruit salad with creamy banana dressing

MAKES 8 SERVINGS

2 cups fresh pineapple chunks

1 cup cantaloupe cubes

1 cup honeydew melon cubes

1 cup fresh blackberries

1 cup sliced fresh strawberries

1 cup seedless red grapes

1 medium apple, diced

2 medium ripe bananas, sliced

½ cup plain or vanilla Greek yogurt

2 tablespoons honey

1 tablespoon fresh lemon juice

¼ teaspoon ground nutmeg

1. Combine pineapple, cantaloupe, honeydew, blackberries, strawberries, grapes and apple in large bowl; mix gently.

2. Combine bananas, yogurt, honey, lemon juice and nutmeg in blender or food processor; blend until smooth.

3. Pour dressing over salad; gently toss to coat. Serve immediately.

farro, chickpea and spinach salad

MAKES 4 TO 6 SERVINGS

1 cup uncooked pearled farro

3 cups baby spinach

1 medium cucumber, chopped

1 can (about 15 ounces) chickpeas, rinsed and drained

¾ cup pitted kalamata olives

¼ cup extra virgin olive oil

3 tablespoons white balsamic vinegar *or* 3 tablespoons cider vinegar mixed with ½ teaspoon sugar

1 teaspoon chopped fresh rosemary

1 clove garlic, minced

1 teaspoon salt

⅛ teaspoon red pepper flakes (optional)

½ cup crumbled goat or feta cheese

1. Bring 4 cups water to a boil in medium saucepan. Add farro; reduce heat and simmer 20 to 25 minutes or until farro is tender. Drain and rinse under cold water until cool.

2. Place farro in large bowl. Add spinach, cucumber, chickpeas and olives.

3. Whisk oil, vinegar, rosemary, garlic, salt and pepper flakes in small bowl. Pour over salad; stir to coat. Gently fold in cheese.

pear arugula salad

MAKES 4 SERVINGS

CARAMELIZED PECANS

- ½ cup pecan halves
- 3 tablespoons packed brown sugar
- 1 tablespoon butter
- 1 tablespoon honey
- ¼ teaspoon salt
- ⅛ teaspoon ground cinnamon

DRESSING

- ¼ cup extra virgin olive oil
- 3 tablespoons balsamic vinegar
- 1 teaspoon pomegranate molasses or honey
- 1 teaspoon Dijon mustard
- ½ teaspoon salt
- ¼ teaspoon dried thyme
- ⅛ teaspoon black pepper

SALAD

- 2 cups arugula
- 2 red pears, thinly sliced
- ½ cup crumbled gorgonzola or blue cheese

1. For pecans, preheat oven to 350°F. Line small baking sheet with foil; spray foil with nonstick cooking spray. Combine pecans, brown sugar, butter, honey, ¼ teaspoon salt and cinnamon in medium skillet. Cook and stir 2 to 3 minutes or until sugar and butter are melted and nuts are glazed. Spread on prepared baking sheet. Bake 5 to 7 minutes or until nuts are fragrant and a shade darker. Remove foil from baking sheet; cool nuts completely on foil.

2. For dressing, whisk oil, vinegar, molasses, mustard, ½ teaspoon salt, thyme and pepper in small bowl until smooth and well blended.

3. Divide arugula among four bowls or plates. Top with pears, nuts and cheese; drizzle with dressing.

NOTE: For a heartier salad, serve with a scoop of cooked red quinoa and top with dried cherries or cranberries.

steakhouse chopped salad

MAKES 8 TO 10 SERVINGS

DRESSING

1½ teaspoons salt

1½ teaspoons dried oregano

¾ teaspoon sugar

¾ teaspoon onion powder

¾ teaspoon dried parsley flakes

½ teaspoon garlic powder

¼ teaspoon dried basil

¼ teaspoon black pepper

⅛ teaspoon dried thyme

⅛ teaspoon celery salt

⅓ cup white balsamic vinegar

¼ cup Dijon mustard

⅔ cup extra virgin olive oil

SALAD

1 head iceberg lettuce, chopped

1 head romaine lettuce, chopped

1 can (about 14 ounces) hearts of palm or artichoke hearts, quartered lengthwise then sliced crosswise

1 large avocado, diced

1½ cups crumbled blue cheese

2 hard-cooked eggs, chopped

1 ripe tomato, chopped

½ red onion, finely chopped

12 slices bacon, crisp-cooked and crumbled

1. For dressing, combine salt, oregano, sugar, onion powder, parsley flakes, garlic powder, basil, pepper, thyme and celery salt in medium bowl. Whisk in vinegar and mustard. Gradually whisk in oil in thin steady stream until well blended. (Dressing can be made up to 1 week in advance; refrigerate in jar with tight-fitting lid.)

2. For salad, combine lettuce, hearts of palm, avocado, cheese, eggs, tomato, onion and bacon in large bowl. Add dressing; toss to coat.

NOTE: This is a huge salad, perfect for large gatherings. Or prepare the ingredients, pack them separately, and then assemble individual servings for lunches and dinners throughout the week.

pecan-crusted chicken salad

MAKES 4 SERVINGS

CHICKEN

- ½ cup all-purpose flour
- ½ cup milk
- 1 egg
- ⅔ cup corn flake crumbs
- ⅔ cup finely chopped pecans
- ¾ teaspoon salt
- 4 boneless skinless chicken breasts (1½ pounds total)

DRESSING

- ⅓ cup balsamic vinegar
- 1 tablespoon Dijon mustard
- 1 tablespoon sugar
- 1 teaspoon minced garlic
- ½ teaspoon salt
- ⅔ cup canola oil

SALAD

- 10 cups mixed greens (1-pound package)
- 2 cans (11 ounces each) mandarin oranges, drained
- 1 cup sliced celery
- ¾ cup dried cranberries
- ½ cup glazed pecans
- ½ cup crumbled blue cheese

1. Preheat oven to 400°F. Line baking sheet with foil; spray with nonstick cooking spray.

2. Place flour in shallow bowl. Whisk milk and egg in another shallow bowl. Combine corn flake crumbs, chopped pecans and salt in third shallow bowl. Dip both sides of chicken in flour, then in egg mixture, letting excess drip back into dish. Roll in crumb mixture to coat completely, pressing crumbs onto chicken to adhere. Place on prepared baking sheet.

3. Bake 20 minutes or until chicken is no longer pink in center. Cool completely before slicing. (Chicken can be prepared several hours in advance and refrigerated.)

4. Meanwhile for dressing, combine vinegar, mustard, sugar, garlic and salt in medium bowl. Gradually whisk in oil in thin steady stream until well blended.

5. For salad, combine mixed greens, oranges, celery, cranberries, glazed pecans and cheese in large bowl. Add two thirds of dressing; toss gently to coat. Divide salad among four plates. Cut chicken breasts diagonally into ½-inch slices; arrange over salads. Serve with remaining dressing.

NOTE: Glazed or candied pecans are often found in the produce section of the supermarket along with other salad convenience items. To make them yourself, follow the directions in step 1 on page 44 for caramelized pecans.

SOUPS & STEWS

celery-leek bisque

MAKES 4 TO 6 SERVINGS

3 bunches leeks (3 pounds), trimmed and well rinsed*

2 cans (about 14 ounces each) vegetable broth

2 stalks celery, sliced

1 carrot, sliced

3 cloves garlic, minced

1 cup cream cheese with garlic and herbs

2 cups half-and-half, plus additional for garnish

Salt and black pepper

Fresh basil leaves (optional)

Thoroughly rinsing the leeks is very important. Gritty sand can get between the layers of the leeks and can be difficult to see, so you may need to rinse them several times.

SLOW COOKER DIRECTIONS

1. Combine leeks, broth, celery, carrot and garlic in 3½-to 4-quart slow cooker. Cover; cook on LOW 8 hours or on HIGH 4 hours.

2. Working in batches, process soup in blender or food processor until smooth. Add cream cheese to last batch. Return to slow cooker. Stir in 2 cups half-and-half. Season with salt and pepper.

3. For best flavor, cool to room temperature and refrigerate overnight. Reheat in large saucepan over medium heat before serving. Garnish with swirl of half-and-half and basil.

tuscan white bean soup

MAKES 8 TO 10 SERVINGS

10 cups chicken or vegetable
  broth

1 package (16 ounces) dried
  Great Northern beans,
  rinsed and sorted

1 can (about 14 ounces) diced
  tomatoes

1 large onion, chopped

3 carrots, chopped

6 ounces bacon, crisp-cooked
  and chopped (optional)

4 cloves garlic, minced

1 sprig fresh rosemary or
  1 teaspoon dried rosemary

1 teaspoon black pepper

SLOW COOKER DIRECTIONS

1. Combine broth, beans, tomatoes, onion, carrots, bacon, if desired, garlic, rosemary and pepper in 5-quart slow cooker.

2. Cover; cook on LOW 8 hours. Remove and discard rosemary before serving.

SERVING SUGGESTION: Place slices of toasted Italian bread in individual soup bowls; drizzle with olive oil. Ladle soup over bread.

curried parsnip soup

MAKES 6 TO 8 SERVINGS

3 pounds parsnips, peeled and cut into 2-inch pieces

1 tablespoon olive oil

2 tablespoons butter

1 medium yellow onion, chopped

2 stalks celery, diced

3 cloves garlic, minced

1 tablespoon salt

1 to 2 teaspoons curry powder

½ teaspoon grated fresh ginger

½ teaspoon black pepper

8 cups vegetable broth

Toasted bread slices (optional)

Chopped fresh chives (optional)

1. Preheat oven to 400°F. Line large baking sheet with foil.

2. Combine parsnips and oil in large bowl; toss to coat. Spread in single layer on prepared baking sheet. Bake 35 to 45 minutes or until parsnips are tender and lightly browned around edges, stirring once halfway through cooking.

3. Melt butter in large saucepan or Dutch oven over medium heat. Add onion and celery; cook and stir about 8 minutes or until vegetables are tender and onion is translucent. Add garlic, salt, curry powder, ginger and pepper; cook and stir 1 minute. Add parsnips and broth; bring to a boil over medium-high heat. Reduce heat to medium-low; cover and simmer 10 minutes.

4. Working in batches, blend soup in blender or food processor until smooth. Ladle into bowls. Serve with toast, if desired; garnish with chives.

cream of broccoli soup

MAKES 8 SERVINGS

1 bunch broccoli (about 1½ pounds), plus additional for garnish

1 medium onion, chopped

1 carrot, chopped

1 stalk celery, chopped

1 potato, peeled and chopped

1 clove garlic, minced

½ teaspoon dried basil

3 cups vegetable broth

2 tablespoons butter

2 tablespoons all-purpose flour

1½ cups milk

1 cup half-and-half

½ teaspoon salt

¼ teaspoon black pepper

½ cup (2 ounces) shredded Cheddar cheese, plus additional for garnish

1. Trim leaves and ends from broccoli stalks. Peel stalks. Cut broccoli into ½-inch pieces.

2. Combine onion, carrot, celery, potato, garlic, basil and broth in large saucepan. Bring to a boil over high heat. Reduce heat to low; simmer 10 minutes. Add broccoli. Simmer 10 minutes or until vegetables are fork-tender. Cool at room temperature 20 to 30 minutes.

3. Process soup in batches in food processor or blender until smooth.

4. Melt butter in Dutch oven over medium heat; whisk in flour until smooth. Cook 1 minute. Gradually whisk in milk and half-and-half. Stir in salt, pepper and ½ cup cheese. Add puréed soup. Cook 3 to 5 minutes until mixture thickens, stirring occasionally.

5. Ladle soup into bowls. Garnish with additional broccoli and cheese.

skillet chicken soup

MAKES 6 SERVINGS

1 teaspoon paprika

½ teaspoon salt

¼ teaspoon black pepper

12 ounces boneless skinless chicken breasts or thighs, cut into ¾-inch pieces

2 teaspoons vegetable oil

1 large onion, chopped

1 red bell pepper, cut into ½-inch pieces

3 cloves garlic, minced

3 cups vegetable broth

1 can (19 ounces) cannellini beans or small white beans, rinsed and drained

3 cups sliced savoy or napa cabbage

Crushed croutons (optional)

1. Combine paprika, salt and black pepper in medium bowl. Add chicken; toss to coat.

2. Heat oil in large deep nonstick skillet over medium-high heat. Add chicken, onion, bell pepper and garlic; cook and stir 8 minutes or until chicken is cooked through.

3. Add broth and beans; bring to a simmer. Cover and simmer 5 minutes. Stir in cabbage; cover and simmer 5 minutes or until cabbage is wilted. Ladle into bowls; top with crushed croutons, if desired.

minestrone soup

MAKES 4 TO 6 SERVINGS

1 tablespoon olive oil

½ cup chopped onion

1 stalk celery, diced

1 carrot, diced

2 cloves garlic, minced

2 cups vegetable broth

1½ cups water

1 bay leaf

¾ teaspoon salt

½ teaspoon dried basil

½ teaspoon dried oregano

¼ teaspoon dried thyme

¼ teaspoon sugar

Ground black pepper

1 can (about 15 ounces) dark red kidney beans, rinsed and drained

1 can (about 15 ounces) navy beans or cannellini beans, rinsed and drained

1 can (about 14 ounces) diced tomatoes

1 cup diced zucchini

½ cup uncooked small shell pasta

½ cup frozen cut green beans

¼ cup dry red wine

1 cup packed chopped fresh spinach

1. Heat oil in large saucepan or Dutch oven over medium-high heat. Add onion, celery, carrot and garlic; cook and stir 5 to 7 minutes or until vegetables are tender. Add broth, water, bay leaf, salt, basil, oregano, thyme, sugar and pepper; bring to a boil.

2. Stir in kidney beans, navy beans, tomatoes, zucchini, pasta, green beans and wine; cook 10 minutes, stirring occasionally.

3. Add spinach; cook 2 minutes or until pasta and zucchini are tender. Ladle into bowls.

black bean soup

MAKES 4 TO 6 SERVINGS

2 tablespoons vegetable oil

1 cup diced onion

1 stalk celery, diced

2 carrots, diced

½ small green bell pepper, diced

4 cloves garlic, minced

4 cans (about 15 ounces each) black beans, rinsed and drained, divided

4 cups (32 ounces) vegetable broth, divided

2 tablespoons cider vinegar

2 teaspoons chili powder

½ teaspoon salt

½ teaspoon ground red pepper

½ teaspoon ground cumin

¼ teaspoon liquid smoke

Garnishes: sour cream, chopped green onions and shredded Cheddar cheese

1. Heat oil in large saucepan or Dutch oven over medium-low heat. Add onion, celery, carrots, bell pepper and garlic; cook 10 minutes, stirring occasionally.

2. Combine half of beans and 1 cup broth in food processor or blender; process until smooth. Add to vegetables in saucepan.

3. Stir in remaining beans, broth, vinegar, chili powder, salt, red pepper, cumin and liquid smoke; bring to a boil over high heat. Reduce heat to medium-low; cook 1 hour or until vegetables are tender and soup is thickened. Garnish as desired.

chickpea and orange squash stew

MAKES 4 SERVINGS

1 tablespoon canola oil

1 yellow onion, chopped

½ to 1 jalapeño pepper, seeded and minced

1 (1-inch) piece fresh ginger, peeled and minced

2 cloves garlic, minced

1 tablespoon ground cumin

1 teaspoon ground coriander

2 cups cubed peeled butternut squash, sweet potato or pumpkin

1 can (about 15 ounces) chickpeas, rinsed and drained

1 cup water

1 tablespoon soy sauce

1 can (about 14 ounces) coconut milk

Juice of 2 limes

½ cup chopped fresh cilantro

1. Heat oil in medium saucepan over medium heat. Add onion, jalapeño pepper, ginger and garlic; cook and stir 2 to 3 minutes or until onion is translucent. Add cumin and coriander; cook and stir 1 minute.

2. Add squash, chickpeas, water and soy sauce to saucepan. Bring to a boil. Reduce heat; simmer 15 minutes or until squash is tender. Add coconut milk; cook and stir 2 to 3 minutes or until heated through. Stir in lime juice and cilantro.

italian escarole and white bean stew

MAKES 4 SERVINGS

1 head escarole (about 12 ounces)

1 tablespoon olive oil

1 onion, chopped

3 carrots, cut into ½-inch-thick rounds

2 cloves garlic, minced

1 can (about 14 ounces) vegetable broth

¼ teaspoon red pepper flakes

2 cans (about 15 ounces each) Great Northern beans, rinsed and drained

Salt

1. Trim base of escarole. Roughly cut crosswise into 1-inch-wide strips. Wash well in large bowl of cold water. Lift out by handfuls, leaving sand or dirt in bottom of bowl. Shake to remove excess water, but do not dry.

2. Heat oil in large saucepan or Dutch oven over medium-high heat. Add onion and carrots; cook and stir about 5 minutes or until onion is softened. Add garlic; cook and stir 1 minute.

3. Add escarole and broth. Sprinkle with red pepper flakes. Top with beans. Bring to a boil. Reduce heat to low. Cover and cook 45 minutes or until escarole is wilted and very tender. Season with salt.

cannellini bean stew with tomatoes and zucchini

MAKES 4 TO 6 SERVINGS

6 plum tomatoes (2 pounds)

4 teaspoons olive oil, divided

1 small onion, chopped

2 cloves garlic, minced

2 cans (about 15 ounces each) cannellini beans, rinsed and drained

2 medium zucchini, cut into ½-inch cubes

2 cups vegetable broth

½ teaspoon dried basil

¼ teaspoon salt

¼ teaspoon black pepper

1. Preheat broiler.

2. Cut tomatoes in half lengthwise; place cut side up in 13×9-inch baking pan. Drizzle with 2 teaspoons oil; broil 12 minutes or until well browned. Cool slightly. Transfer tomatoes to food processor; pulse until coarsely chopped.

3. Meanwhile, heat remaining 2 teaspoons oil in large saucepan over medium-high heat. Add onion; cook and stir 3 minutes. Add garlic; cook and stir 1 minute. Add beans, zucchini, broth, tomatoes, basil, salt and pepper. Bring to a boil. Reduce heat. Cover and simmer 8 minutes or just until zucchini is tender.

vegetarian quinoa chili

MAKES 4 TO 6 SERVINGS

2 tablespoons vegetable oil

1 large onion, diced

1 red bell pepper, diced

1 large carrot, diced

1 stalk celery, diced

1 jalapeño pepper, seeded and finely chopped

1 tablespoon minced garlic

3 tablespoons chili powder

2 teaspoons ground cumin

2 teaspoons salt

1 can (about 15 ounces) kidney beans, rinsed and drained

1 can (28 ounces) crushed tomatoes

1 cup water

1 cup corn

½ cup uncooked quinoa, rinsed well in fine-mesh strainer

Garnishes: diced avocado, shredded Cheddar cheese and sliced green onions

1. Heat oil in large saucepan over medium-high heat. Add onion, bell pepper, carrot and celery; cook about 10 minutes until softened, stirring occasionally. Add jalapeño pepper, garlic, chili powder, cumin and salt; cook about 1 minute or until fragrant.

2. Add beans, tomatoes, water, corn and quinoa; bring to a boil. Reduce heat to low; cover and simmer 1 hour, stirring occasionally.

3. Spoon into bowls; garnish as desired.

ribollita
(tuscan bread soup)

MAKES 6 TO 8 SERVINGS

2 tablespoons olive oil

1 onion, halved and thinly sliced

2 stalks celery, diced

1 large carrot, julienned

3 cloves garlic, minced

2 medium zucchini, halved lengthwise and thinly sliced

1 medium yellow squash, halved lengthwise and thinly sliced

1 can (28 ounces) whole tomatoes, undrained

1 can (about15 ounces) cannellini beans, rinsed and drained

1½ teaspoons salt

1 teaspoon Italian seasoning

¼ teaspoon black pepper

1 bay leaf

¼ teaspoon red pepper flakes

4 cups vegetable broth

2 cups water

1 bunch kale, stemmed and coarsely chopped *or* 3 cups thinly sliced cabbage

8 ounces Tuscan or other rustic bread, cubed

1. Heat oil in large saucepan over medium-high heat. Add onion, celery and carrot; cook and stir 5 minutes. Add garlic, zucchini and yellow squash; cook and stir 5 minutes.

2. Add tomatoes, beans, salt, Italian seasoning, black pepper, bay leaf and red pepper flakes. Add broth and water; bring to a boil. Reduce heat; simmer 15 minutes.

3. Add kale and bread; simmer 10 minutes or until vegetables are tender, bread is soft and soup is thick.

NOTE: This is a great recipe to use a spiralizer if you have one. Use the spiral slicing blade to spiral the zucchini and yellow squash, then cut in half to make half moon slices. Use the thin ribbon blade to spiral the onion and carrot, and then cut into desired lengths.

pozole

MAKES 6 SERVINGS

1 large onion, thinly sliced

1 tablespoon olive oil

2 teaspoons dried oregano

1 clove garlic, minced

½ teaspoon ground cumin

2 cans (about 14 ounces each) chicken broth

1 package (10 ounces) frozen corn

2 cans (4 ounces each) chopped green chiles, undrained

1 can (2¼ ounces) sliced black olives, drained

12 ounces boneless skinless chicken breasts

Chopped fresh cilantro (optional)

1. Combine onion, oil, oregano, garlic and cumin in Dutch oven. Cover and cook over low heat about 6 minutes or until onion is tender, stirring occasionally.

2. Stir in broth, corn, chiles and olives. Cover and bring to a boil over high heat.

3. Meanwhile, cut chicken into thin strips. Add to soup. Reduce heat to medium-low; cover and cook 3 to 4 minutes or until chicken is no longer pink. Garnish with cilantro, if desired.

BOWLS

greek salad bowl

MAKES 4 SERVINGS

1 cup uncooked pearled farro

2½ cups water

1¼ teaspoons dried oregano or Greek seasoning, divided

½ teaspoon salt, divided

¼ cup extra virgin olive oil

2 tablespoons red wine vinegar

1 clove garlic, minced

⅛ teaspoon black pepper (optional)

2 cucumbers, julienned, cubed or thinly sliced

½ red onion, thinly sliced

2 medium tomatoes, diced

1 can (about 15 ounces) chickpeas, rinsed and drained

4 ounces feta cheese, cubed or crumbled

1. Rinse farro under cold water; place in medium saucepan. Add 2½ cups water, 1 teaspoon oregano and ¼ teaspoon salt. Bring to a boil over high heat. Reduce heat to medium-low; simmer, uncovered, 20 minutes or until farro is tender. Drain any additional water.

2. Whisk oil, vinegar, garlic, remaining ¼ teaspoon salt, remaining ¼ teaspoon oregano and pepper, if desired, in small bowl.

3. Divide farro among four bowls; top with cucumbers, onion, tomatoes, chickpeas and cheese. Drizzle with dressing.

NOTE: This is a great recipe to use a spiralizer if you have one. Cut the ends off the cucumbers and spiral slice with the thin ribbon blade. Spiral the red onion with the thin ribbon blade and chop into desired pieces.

sweet potato noodles with blue cheese and walnuts

MAKES 2 SERVINGS

2 sweet potatoes (1½ pounds), peeled

¼ cup chopped walnuts

1 tablespoon olive oil

¼ teaspoon salt

¼ teaspoon black pepper

2 cloves garlic, minced

1 package (5 ounces) baby spinach

¼ cup heavy cream

¼ cup crumbled blue cheese

1. Using a spiralizer, spiral sweet potatoes with thin ribbon blade. Loosely pile on cutting board and cut in an X.

2. Heat large nonstick skillet over medium-high heat. Add walnuts; cook and stir 3 to 4 minutes until toasted. Remove to plate; cool completely.

3. Heat oil in same skillet over medium-high heat. Add sweet potatoes, ¼ teaspoon salt and ¼ teaspoon pepper; cook and stir 10 minutes or until desired doneness, adding water by tablespoonfuls if sweet potatoes are browning too quickly.

4. Add garlic; cook and stir 30 seconds. Add cream and spinach; cook and stir 1 minute or until cream is absorbed and spinach is wilted. Transfer to bowls; top with walnuts and cheese. Season with additional salt and pepper.

tofu satay bowl

MAKES 4 SERVINGS

1 package (about 14 ounces) firm or extra firm tofu, drained and pressed*

⅓ cup water

⅓ cup soy sauce

1 tablespoon dark sesame oil

1 teaspoon minced garlic

1 teaspoon minced fresh ginger

24 white or cremini mushrooms, trimmed

1 red bell pepper, cut into 12 pieces

Cucumber Relish (page 79)

1 cup uncooked jasmine rice, cooked according to package directions

PEANUT SAUCE

1 can (about 14 ounces) unsweetened coconut milk

½ cup creamy peanut butter

2 tablespoons packed brown sugar

1 tablespoon rice vinegar

2 teaspoons red Thai curry paste

If you use extra firm silken tofu, there is no need to press it.

1. Cut tofu into 24 cubes. Combine water, soy sauce, sesame oil, garlic and ginger in small bowl. Place tofu, mushrooms and bell pepper in large resealable food storage bag. Add soy sauce mixture. Seal bag; turn to coat. Marinate 30 minutes, turning occasionally. Soak eight 8-inch bamboo skewers in cold water 20 minutes. Meanwhile, prepare cucumber relish.

2. Preheat oven to 400°F. Spray 13×9-inch baking pan with nonstick cooking spray. Drain tofu mixture; discard marinade. Thread tofu and vegetables alternately onto skewers; place in prepared baking pan. Bake 25 minutes or until tofu cubes are lightly browned and vegetables are softened.

3. Meanwhile for peanut sauce, whisk coconut milk, peanut butter, brown sugar, vinegar and curry paste in small saucepan over medium heat. Bring to a boil, stirring constantly. Immediately reduce heat to low. Cook about 20 minutes or until creamy and thick, stirring frequently. Serve tofu, vegetables and sauce over rice with cucumber relish.

cucumber relish

MAKES 4 SERVINGS

¼ cup rice vinegar

2 tablespoons granulated sugar

¼ teaspoon salt

1 cucumber, halved lengthwise
  and thinly sliced

½ red onion, thinly sliced

1 large carrot, shredded or
  julienned

1. Heat vinegar, sugar and salt in small saucepan until sugar is dissolved. Pour into large bowl; cool completely.

2. Add vegetables to vinegar mixture. Serve immediately or refrigerate until ready to serve.

pepper and egg couscous bowl

MAKES 4 SERVINGS

1 tablespoon olive oil

3 bell peppers, assorted colors, thinly sliced

1 red onion, thinly sliced

2 cups vegetable broth

1 cup uncooked instant couscous

1 clove garlic, minced

½ teaspoon salt

½ teaspoon dried oregano

½ teaspoon ground cumin

4 to 8 eggs, cooked any style

1 can (about 15 ounces) black beans, rinsed and drained

1 cup grape tomatoes, halved

Crumbled queso fresco, cotija or feta cheese (optional)

1. Heat oil in large skillet over medium-high heat. Add bell peppers and onion; cook and stir 5 minutes or until vegetables are tender.

2. Bring broth to a boil in small saucepan. Stir in couscous, garlic, salt, oregano and cumin. Remove from heat. Cover and let stand 5 minutes. Fluff with fork.

3. Serve vegetables, eggs, beans and tomatoes over couscous; top with cheese, if desired.

salmon and rice bowl

MAKES 4 SERVINGS

RICE

- 1 cup uncooked long grain brown rice or sushi rice
- 1 teaspoon rice vinegar

SAUCE

- ¼ cup mayonnaise
- 1 tablespoon chopped fresh cilantro
- 1 clove garlic, minced
- ½ teaspoon sriracha sauce
- 2 to 3 teaspoons lime juice

SALMON

- 2 tablespoons orange juice
- 2 tablespoons soy sauce
- 1 tablespoon honey
- ¾ teaspoon grated fresh ginger
- ½ teaspoon rice vinegar
- ¼ teaspoon dark sesame oil
- 4 salmon fillets (6 ounces each)
- ¼ teaspoon black pepper
- 1 tablespoon olive oil

TOPPINGS

- 2 small cucumbers
- 1 large carrot, peeled
- 1 cup shelled edamame
- 1 avocado, thinly sliced
- 1 jalapeño pepper, seeded and sliced

1. Cook rice according to package directions. Stir in 1 teaspoon vinegar; set aside.

2. For sauce, combine mayonnaise, 1 tablespoon cilantro, garlic and sriracha in small bowl. Stir in lime juice to taste. Refrigerate until ready to serve.

3. For salmon, whisk orange juice, soy sauce, honey, ginger, ½ teaspoon vinegar and sesame oil in small bowl. Season salmon with pepper. Heat olive oil in large nonstick skillet over medium-high heat. Place salmon skin side up in skillet; brush with glaze. Cook 4 minutes or just until center is opaque. Carefully turn; brush with some of remaining glaze. Cook 4 minutes or until salmon begins to flake when tested with fork. If desired, cook remaining glaze in small saucepan until thickened and reduced to 2 tablespoons.

4. Using spiralizer, spiral cucumbers and carrot with thin ribbon blade; cut into 3-inch lengths.

5. Divide rice among four bowls. Arrange cucumbers, carrot, edamame, avocado and jalapeño pepper in bowl. Top with salmon; serve with sauce and glaze, if desired.

smoky chili with corn-cilantro quinoa

MAKES 8 SERVINGS

CHILI

- 1 tablespoon canola oil
- 1 pound ground beef or turkey
- 2 cups coarsely chopped green bell peppers
- 1 cup coarsely chopped onion
- 2 cans (about 14 ounces each) stewed tomatoes
- 2 cans (about 15 ounces each) dark kidney beans, rinsed and drained
- 2½ cups water
- 2 teaspoons smoked paprika
- 3 teaspoons ground cumin, divided
  Salt and pepper

QUINOA

- 1 cup uncooked tri-color or white quinoa
- 2 cups water
- ½ teaspoon salt
- 1½ cups frozen corn
- ½ cup chopped fresh cilantro
- 1 cup sour cream

1. Heat oil in Dutch oven over medium-high heat. Add beef; cook 3 minutes or until just beginning to brown, stirring frequently. Stir in bell peppers and onion; cook 6 minutes or until vegetables are just tender.

2. Stir in tomatoes, beans, water, paprika and 1 teaspoon cumin. Bring to a boil. Reduce heat to medium-low; cook 30 minutes or until thickened. Remove from heat; stir in remaining 2 teaspoons cumin. Season with salt and pepper.

3. Meanwhile, place quinoa in fine-mesh strainer; rinse well under cold water. Combine quinoa, 2 cups water and ½ teaspoon salt in medium saucepan; bring to a boil over high heat. Reduce heat to low; cover and simmer 15 to 18 minutes or until quinoa is tender and water is absorbed, adding corn during last few minutes of cooking. Fluff with fork; stir in cilantro.

4. Spoon quinoa mixture into bowls; top with chili and sour cream.

california roll farro
sushi bowl

MAKES 4 SERVINGS

1 cup uncooked pearled farro

2½ cups water

2 tablespoons unseasoned rice vinegar

2 tablespoons sugar

½ teaspoon salt, divided

1 cup shredded carrots

2 avocados, sliced

2 mini (kirby) cucumbers, thinly sliced

12 ounces crab sticks or imitation crab sticks

2 teaspoons toasted sesame seeds

DRESSING

⅓ cup mayonnaise

1 teaspoon sriracha sauce

1 teaspoon dark sesame oil

1 teaspoon rice vinegar

1. Rinse farro under cold water; place in medium saucepan. Add 2½ cups water and ¼ teaspoon salt. Bring to a boil over high heat. Reduce heat to medium-low; simmer, uncovered, 20 minutes or until farro is tender. Drain any additional water.

2. Combine 2 tablespoons rice vinegar, sugar and remaining ¼ teaspoon salt in large microwavable bowl. Microwave on HIGH 30 to 45 seconds; stir to combine. Add farro; toss well.

3. Divide farro mixture evenly among four bowls. Top evenly with carrots, avocados, cucumbers and crab sticks. Sprinkle with sesame seeds.

4. Whisk mayonnaise, sriracha sauce, sesame oil and 1 teaspoon rice vinegar in small bowl. Serve on the side or thin with water and drizzle over the top.

roasted chickpea and sweet potato bowl

MAKES 2 SERVINGS

1 sweet potato (about 12 ounces)

1 tablespoon plus 1 teaspoon olive oil, divided

1 teaspoon salt, divided

Black pepper

1 can (about 15 ounces) chickpeas, rinsed and drained

1 tablespoon maple syrup

1 teaspoon paprika, sweet or smoked

½ teaspoon ground cumin

½ cup uncooked quinoa, rinsed well in fine-mesh strainer

Chopped fresh parsley or cilantro

TAHINI SAUCE

¼ cup tahini

2 tablespoons lemon juice

2 tablespoons water

1 clove garlic, minced

⅛ teaspoon salt

1. Preheat oven to 350°F.

2. Peel sweet potato and cut in half. Using a spiralizer, spiral sweet potato with thin ribbon blade. Cut into 3-inch pieces. Place in 13×9-inch baking pan. Drizzle with 1 teaspoon oil and sprinkle with ¼ teaspoon salt and black pepper; toss to coat. Push to one side of pan.

3. Combine chickpeas, maple syrup, remaining 1 tablespoon oil, paprika, cumin and ½ teaspoon salt in medium bowl; toss to coat. Spread in other side of pan. Bake 30 minutes, stirring potatoes and chickpeas once or twice.

4. Meanwhile, bring quinoa, 1 cup water and ¼ teaspoon salt to a boil in small saucepan. Reduce heat to low; cover and simmer 15 minutes or until quinoa is tender and water is absorbed.

5. For sauce, whisk tahini, lemon juice, 2 tablespoons water, garlic and ⅛ teaspoon salt in small bowl until smooth. Add additional water if needed to reach desired consistency.

6. Divide quinoa between two bowls. Top with sweet potatoes, chickpeas and sauce. Sprinkle with parsley.

NOTE: If you don't have a spiralizer, julienne the sweet potato or cut it into cubes instead.

rosemary, haricots verts and goat cheese quinoa

MAKES 6 SERVINGS

1 cup uncooked tri-colored quinoa

2 cups vegetable broth

1 tablespoon chopped fresh rosemary

1 package (12 ounces) fresh haricots verts or green beans, cut in half

3 tablespoons extra virgin olive oil

1 tablespoon Dijon mustard

1 tablespoon fresh lemon juice

1 teaspoon honey

¼ teaspoon salt

⅛ teaspoon black pepper

½ cup toasted pecan pieces

1 container (4 ounces) goat cheese crumbles

1. Place quinoa in fine-mesh strainer; rinse well under cold water.

2. Combine quinoa and broth in medium saucepan; bring to a boil over high heat. Reduce heat to low; cover and simmer 15 to 20 minutes or until quinoa is tender and broth is absorbed. Add rosemary and haricots verts during last 5 minutes of cooking. Remove from heat; cool slightly.

3. Meanwhile, combine oil, mustard, lemon juice, honey, salt and pepper in small bowl; set aside.

4. Place cooled quinoa mixture in large bowl. Toss with dressing and pecans. Sprinkle with goat cheese before serving.

MEAT & FISH

forty-clove chicken filice

MAKES 4 TO 6 SERVINGS

¼ cup olive oil

1 whole chicken (about 3 pounds), cut into serving pieces

40 cloves garlic (about 2 heads), peeled

4 stalks celery, thickly sliced

½ cup dry white wine

¼ cup dry vermouth

Grated peel and juice of 1 lemon

2 tablespoons finely chopped fresh parsley

2 teaspoons dried basil

1 teaspoon dried oregano, crushed

Pinch of red pepper flakes

Salt and black pepper

1. Preheat oven to 375°F.

2. Heat oil in Dutch oven. Add chicken; cook until browned on all sides.

3. Combine garlic, celery, wine, vermouth, lemon juice, parsley, basil, oregano and red pepper flakes in medium bowl; pour over chicken. Sprinkle with lemon peel; season with salt and black pepper.

4. Cover and bake 40 minutes. Remove cover; bake 15 minutes or until chicken is cooked through (165°F).

shrimp tacos

MAKES 8 SERVINGS

1 pound jumbo or colossal raw shrimp, peeled and deveined (16 count)

2 tablespoons fresh lemon juice, divided

½ teaspoon ground cumin, divided

¼ teaspoon black pepper

1 pint cherry or grape tomatoes, halved

1 small red onion, finely chopped

1 serrano pepper, cored, seeded and minced

1 clove garlic, minced

1 tablespoon chopped fresh cilantro

¼ teaspoon salt

8 taco shells or corn tortillas, heated

1 cup coarsely shredded romaine lettuce

1 small avocado, cut into 8 wedges

1. Cut shrimp along the vein to butterfly. Place in large glass bowl with 1 tablespoon lemon juice, ¼ teaspoon cumin and black pepper. Stir well. Let stand 30 minutes.

2. Meanwhile, for salsa, combine tomatoes, onion, serrano pepper, garlic, cilantro, remaining 1 tablespoon lemon juice, remaining ¼ teaspoon cumin and salt in small bowl. Stir well; set aside.

3. Spray large skillet with nonstick cooking spray over medium heat 30 seconds. Cook shrimp in batches (do not crowd pan) 3 to 4 minutes on each side or until cooked through.

4. Place 2 shrimp in each taco shell. Add 2 tablespoons salsa, 2 tablespoons lettuce and 1 avocado wedge. Serve remaining salsa on the side.

roast chicken and potatoes catalan

MAKES 4 SERVINGS

2 tablespoons olive oil

2 tablespoons lemon juice

1 teaspoon dried thyme

½ teaspoon salt

¼ teaspoon ground red pepper

¼ teaspoon ground saffron *or* ½ teaspoon crushed saffron threads or turmeric

2 large baking potatoes (about 1½ pounds), cut into 1½-inch chunks

4 skinless bone-in chicken breasts (about 2 pounds)

1 cup sliced red bell pepper

1 cup frozen peas, thawed

Lemon wedges (optional)

1. Preheat oven to 400°F. Spray large shallow roasting pan or 15×10-inch baking sheet with nonstick cooking spray.

2. Combine oil, lemon juice, thyme, salt, ground red pepper and saffron in large bowl; mix well. Add potatoes; toss to coat.

3. Arrange potatoes in single layer around edges of pan. Place chicken in center of pan; brush both sides of chicken with remaining oil mixture in bowl.

4. Bake 20 minutes. Turn potatoes; baste chicken with pan juices. Add bell pepper; continue baking 20 minutes or until chicken is no longer pink in center, juices run clear and potatoes are browned. Stir peas into potato mixture; bake 5 minutes or until heated through. Serve with lemon wedges, if desired.

italian-style pot roast

MAKES 6 TO 8 SERVINGS

2 teaspoons minced garlic

1 teaspoon salt

1 teaspoon dried basil

1 teaspoon dried oregano

¼ teaspoon red pepper flakes

1 boneless beef bottom round or chuck roast (2½ to 3 pounds)

1 onion, quartered and thinly sliced

1½ cups tomato sauce or marinara pasta sauce

2 cans (about 15 ounces each) cannellini or Great Northern beans, rinsed and drained

¼ cup thinly sliced fresh basil

SLOW COOKER DIRECTIONS

1. Combine garlic, salt, dried basil, oregano and red pepper flakes in small bowl; rub over roast.

2. Place half of onion slices in slow cooker. Cut roast in half crosswise. Place half of roast over onion slices; top with remaining onion slices and other half of roast. Pour tomato sauce over roast. Cover; cook on LOW 8 to 9 hours or until roast is fork-tender.

3. Remove roast to cutting board; tent with foil. Let liquid in slow cooker stand 5 minutes. Skim off fat.

4. *Turn slow cooker to HIGH.* Stir beans into liquid. Cover; cook 15 to 30 minutes or until beans are heated through. Carve roast across the grain into thin slices. Serve with bean mixture and fresh basil.

chicken cassoulet

MAKES 6 SERVINGS

4 slices bacon

¼ cup all-purpose flour
  Salt and black pepper

1¾ pounds bone-in chicken
  pieces

2 chicken sausages (2¼ ounces
  each), cooked and cut into
  ¼-inch pieces

1 medium onion, chopped

1½ cups diced red and green bell
  peppers

2 cloves garlic, minced

1 teaspoon dried thyme

1 teaspoon olive oil

½ cup dry white wine

2 cans (about 15 ounces each)
  cannellini or Great Northern
  beans, rinsed and drained

1. Preheat oven to 350°F.

2. Cook bacon in Dutch oven over medium-high heat until crisp; drain on paper towels. Cut into 1-inch pieces. Pour off all but 2 tablespoons drippings.

3. Place flour in shallow bowl; season with salt and black pepper. Dip chicken pieces in flour mixture; shake off excess. Brown chicken in batches in Dutch oven over medium-high heat; remove to plate. Lightly brown sausages in same Dutch oven; remove to plate.

4. Add onion, bell peppers, garlic and thyme to Dutch oven; cook and stir over medium heat 5 minutes or until softened, adding oil as needed to prevent sticking. Add wine; cook and stir over medium heat, scraping up browned bits from bottom of pan. Add beans; mix well. Top with chicken, sausages and bacon.

5. Bake, covered, 40 minutes. Remove cover; bake 15 minutes or until chicken is cooked through (165°F).

miso salmon

MAKES 4 SERVINGS

1 **cup uncooked long grain rice**

4 **salmon fillets (about 6 ounces each)**

¼ **cup packed brown sugar**

¼ **cup red or white miso**

2 **tablespoons soy sauce**

1 **tablespoon hot water**

1 **tablespoon butter**

1 **tablespoon minced fresh ginger**

1 **tablespoon minced shallot or red onion**

½ **cup plus 1 teaspoon sake, divided**

1 **tablespoon whipping cream or half-and-half**

½ **cup (1 stick) cold butter, cut into small pieces**

1 **teaspoon lime juice**

½ **teaspoon salt**

2 **green onions, cut into julienne strips**

1. Cook rice according to package directions; keep warm.

2. Preheat broiler. Spray 13×9-inch baking pan with nonstick cooking spray. Place salmon in prepared pan.

3. Whisk brown sugar, miso, soy sauce and hot water in small bowl until well blended. Spoon half of mixture evenly over fish. Broil 10 minutes or until fish begins to flake when tested with fork, spooning remaining mixture over fish twice during cooking.

4. Meanwhile, melt 1 tablespoon butter in small saucepan over medium heat. Add ginger and shallot; cook and stir 3 minutes or until softened. Add ½ cup sake; bring to a boil over medium-high heat. Cook 3 to 5 minutes or until reduced to 2 tablespoons. Whisk in cream. Add cold butter, one piece at a time, whisking constantly until butter is incorporated before adding next piece. Remove from heat; whisk in remaining 1 teaspoon sake, lime juice and ½ teaspoon salt. Season with additional salt, if desired.

5. Spread sauce on four plates; top with rice, fish and green onions.

crispy roasted chicken

MAKES 8 TO 10 SERVINGS

1 roasting chicken or capon (about 6½ pounds)

1 tablespoon peanut or vegetable oil

2 cloves garlic, minced

1 tablespoon soy sauce

1. Preheat oven to 350°F. Place chicken on rack in shallow, foil-lined roasting pan.

2. Combine oil and garlic in small cup; brush evenly over chicken. Roast 15 to 20 minutes per pound or until internal temperature reaches 170°F when tested with meat thermometer inserted into thickest part of thigh not touching bone.

3. *Increase oven temperature to 450°F.* Remove drippings from pan; discard. Brush chicken evenly with soy sauce. Roast 5 to 10 minutes until skin is very crisp and deep golden brown.

4. Transfer chicken to cutting board; let stand 10 to 15 minutes before carving. Internal temperature will continue to rise 5° to 10°F during stand time.

steak fajitas

MAKES 2 SERVINGS

¼ cup lime juice

¼ cup soy sauce

4 tablespoons vegetable oil, divided

2 tablespoons honey

2 tablespoons Worcestershire sauce

2 cloves garlic, minced

½ teaspoon ground red pepper

1 pound flank steak, skirt steak or top sirloin

1 medium yellow onion, halved and cut into ¼-inch slices

1 green bell pepper, cut into ¼-inch strips

1 red bell pepper, cut into ¼-inch strips

Flour tortillas, warmed

Lime wedges (optional)

Toppings: pico de gallo, guacamole, sour cream, shredded lettuce and shredded Cheddar-Jack cheese

1. Combine lime juice, soy sauce, 2 tablespoons oil, honey, Worcestershire sauce, garlic and ground red pepper in medium bowl; mix well. Remove ¼ cup marinade to large bowl. Place steak in large resealable food storage bag. Pour remaining marinade over steak; seal bag and turn to coat. Marinate in refrigerator at least 2 hours or overnight. Add onion and bell peppers to bowl with ¼ cup marinade; toss to coat. Cover and refrigerate until ready to use.

2. Remove steak from marinade; discard marinade and wipe off excess from steak. Heat 1 tablespoon oil in large skillet (preferably cast iron) over medium-high heat. Cook steak about 4 minutes per side for medium rare or to desired doneness. Remove to cutting board; tent with foil and let rest 10 minutes.

3. Meanwhile, heat remaining 1 tablespoon oil in same skillet over medium-high heat. Add vegetable mixture; cook about 8 minutes or until vegetables are crisp-tender and beginning to brown in spots, stirring occasionally. (Cook in batches if necessary; do not pile vegetables in skillet.)

4. Cut steak into thin slices across the grain. Serve with vegetables, tortillas, lime wedges and desired toppings.

chicken scarpiello

MAKES 4 TO 6 SERVINGS

3 tablespoons extra virgin olive oil, divided

1 pound spicy Italian sausage, cut into 1-inch pieces

1 cut-up whole chicken (about 3 pounds)*

1 teaspoon salt, divided

1 large onion, chopped

2 red, yellow or orange bell peppers, cut into ¼-inch strips

3 cloves garlic, minced

½ cup dry white wine such as sauvignon blanc

½ cup chicken broth

½ cup coarsely chopped seeded hot cherry peppers

½ cup liquid from cherry pepper jar

1 teaspoon dried oregano

Additional salt and black pepper

¼ cup chopped fresh Italian parsley

*Or purchase 2 bone-in chicken leg quarters and 2 chicken breasts; separate drumsticks and thighs and cut breasts in half.

1. Heat 1 tablespoon oil in large skillet over medium-high heat. Add sausage; cook about 10 minutes or until well browned on all sides, stirring occasionally. Remove sausage from skillet; set aside.

2. Heat 1 tablespoon oil in same skillet. Sprinkle chicken with ½ teaspoon salt; arrange skin side down in single layer in skillet (cook in batches if necessary). Cook about 6 minutes per side or until browned. Remove chicken from skillet; set aside. Drain oil from skillet.

3. Heat remaining 1 tablespoon oil in skillet. Add onion and remaining ½ teaspoon salt; cook and stir 2 minutes or until onion is softened, scraping up browned bits from bottom of skillet. Add bell peppers and garlic; cook and stir 5 minutes. Stir in wine; cook until liquid is reduced by half. Stir in broth, cherry peppers, cherry pepper liquid, oregano and salt and black pepper to taste; bring to a simmer.

4. Return sausage and chicken along with any accumulated juices to skillet. Partially cover skillet and simmer 10 minutes. Uncover and simmer 15 minutes or until chicken is cooked through (165°F). Sprinkle with parsley.

TIP: If too much liquid remains in the skillet when the chicken is cooked through, remove the chicken and sausage and continue simmering the sauce to reduce it slightly.

chicken with rosemary-peach glaze

MAKES 4 SERVINGS

4 boneless skinless chicken breasts (about 1 pound)

2 tablespoons soy sauce, divided

⅓ cup peach preserves

1 sprig fresh rosemary *or* 1 teaspoon dried rosemary

1 tablespoon lemon juice

1 clove garlic, minced

1. Preheat broiler. Spray baking sheet with nonstick cooking spray. Sprinkle chicken with 1 tablespoon soy sauce; place on prepared baking sheet. Broil 4 to 6 inches from heat 3 minutes; turn and broil 3 minutes longer.

2. Meanwhile, combine preserves, rosemary, lemon juice, remaining 1 tablespoon soy sauce and garlic in small saucepan. Cook over medium-low heat 5 minutes.

3. Brush sauce over chicken; broil 2 minutes. Turn and brush with sauce. Broil 2 minutes longer or until chicken is no longer pink in center.

pork chops with bell peppers and sweet potato

MAKES 4 SERVINGS

4 pork loin chops (about 1 pound), cut about ½ inch thick

1 teaspoon lemon-pepper seasoning

½ cup water

1 tablespoon lemon juice

1 teaspoon dried fines herbes, crushed

½ teaspoon beef bouillon granules

1¼ cups red or yellow bell pepper strips or a combination

1 cup sliced sweet potato, cut into 1-inch pieces

¾ cup sliced onion

1. Trim fat from chops; discard. Rub both sides of chops with lemon-pepper seasoning. Coat large skillet with nonstick cooking spray. Heat skillet over medium-high heat. Add chops; cook 5 minutes or until browned on both sides.

2. Combine water, lemon juice, fines herbes and bouillon granules in small bowl; stir to blend. Pour over chops. Reduce heat to medium-low. Cover; simmer 5 minutes.

3. Add bell pepper, sweet potato and onion to skillet; return to a boil. Reduce heat. Cover; simmer 10 to 15 minutes or until chops are slightly pink in center and vegetables are crisp-tender. Remove chops and vegetables from skillet; keep warm.

4. Bring remaining juices in skillet to a boil over high heat. Reduce heat to medium. Cook and stir 6 to 8 minutes or until mixture slightly thickens, stirring occasionally. Arrange chops and vegetables on large serving plate; spoon sauce over chops and vegetables.

honey-roasted chicken and butternut squash

MAKES 4 TO 6 SERVINGS

1 **pound fresh butternut squash chunks**

Salt and black pepper

6 **bone-in chicken thighs**

1 **tablespoon honey**

1. Preheat oven to 375°F. Spray baking sheet and wire rack with nonstick cooking spray.

2. Spread squash on prepared baking sheet; season with salt and pepper.

3. Place wire rack over squash; place chicken on rack. Season with salt and pepper.

4. Roast 25 minutes. Carefully lift rack and stir squash; brush honey over chicken pieces. Roast 20 minutes or until chicken is cooked through (165°F).

pineapple-hoisin hens

MAKES 4 SERVINGS

2 cloves garlic

1 can (8 ounces) crushed pineapple in juice, undrained

2 tablespoons rice vinegar

2 tablespoons soy sauce

2 tablespoons hoisin sauce

2 teaspoons minced fresh ginger

1 teaspoon Chinese five-spice powder

2 large Cornish hens (about 1½ pounds each), split in half

1. Mince garlic in blender or food processor. Add pineapple with juice; process until fairly smooth. Add vinegar, soy sauce, hoisin sauce, ginger and five-spice powder; process 5 seconds.

2. Place hens in large resealable food storage bag; pour pineapple mixture over hens. Seal bag; turn to coat. Marinate in refrigerator at least 2 hours or up to 24 hours, turning bag once.

3. Preheat oven to 375°F. Drain hens; reserve marinade. Place hens, skin side up, on rack in shallow, foil-lined roasting pan. Roast 35 minutes.

4. Brush hens lightly with some reserved marinade; discard remaining marinade. Roast 10 minutes or until hens are browned and cooked through (180°F).

shredded beef tacos

MAKES 6 TO 8 SERVINGS

1 boneless beef chuck roast (2½ pounds)

1¼ teaspoons salt, divided

1 teaspoon *each* cumin, garlic powder and smoked paprika

2 tablespoons olive oil, divided

2 cups beef broth

1 red bell pepper, sliced

1 tomato, cut into wedges

½ onion, sliced

2 cloves garlic, minced

1 to 2 canned chipotle peppers in adobo sauce

Juice of 1 lime

Corn or flour tortillas

Toppings: sliced bell peppers, avocado, diced onion, lime wedges and/or chopped fresh cilantro

SLOW COOKER DIRECTIONS

1. Season beef with 1 teaspoon salt, cumin, garlic powder and paprika. Heat 1 tablespoon oil in large skillet over medium-high heat. Add beef; cook 5 minutes on each side until browned. Transfer to slow cooker.

2. Pour in broth. Cover; cook on LOW 8 to 9 hours or on HIGH 4 to 5 hours.

3. Meanwhile, preheat oven to 425°F. Combine bell pepper, tomato, onion and garlic on large baking sheet. Drizzle with remaining 1 tablespoon oil. Roast 40 minutes or until vegetables are tender. Place vegetables, chipotle pepper, lime juice and remaining ¼ teaspoon salt in food processor or blender; blend until smooth.

4. Transfer beef to large cutting board; shred with two forks. Combine shredded meat with 1 cup cooking liquid. Discard remaining cooking liquid. Serve on tortillas with sauce and desired toppings.

VEGETARIAN

southwestern flatbread with black beans and corn

MAKES 4 SERVINGS

¼ cup prepared green chile enchilada sauce

2 oval flatbreads (about 7×11 inches)

2 cups (8 ounces) shredded Monterey Jack cheese

1 can (about 14 ounces) black beans, rinsed and drained

1 cup corn

½ cup finely diced red onion

½ teaspoon salt

1 teaspoon extra virgin olive oil

2 tablespoons fresh chopped cilantro

1 avocado, diced

Lime wedges (optional)

1. Preheat oven to 425°F. Place wire rack on top of baking sheet.

2. Spread enchilada sauce evenly on top of each flatbread, sprinkle evenly with cheese. Combine beans, corn, onion, salt and oil in medium bowl. Layer mixture on top of cheese. Place flatbreads on rack on baking sheet.

3. Bake 12 minutes or until flatbreads are golden and crisp, and cheese is melted. Remove from oven. Sprinkle with cilantro and avocado.

4. Cut each flatbread crosswise into four pieces. Serve with lime wedges, if desired.

mediterranean vegetable sandwich

MAKES 4 SANDWICHES

½ cup plain hummus

½ jalapeño pepper, seeded and minced

¼ cup minced fresh cilantro

8 slices whole wheat bread

4 leaves lettuce (leaf or Bibb lettuce)

2 tomatoes, thinly sliced

½ cucumber, thinly sliced

½ red onion, thinly sliced

½ cup thinly sliced peppadew peppers or sweet Italian peppers

4 tablespoons crumbled feta cheese

1. Combine hummus, jalapeño and cilantro in small bowl; mix well.

2. Spread about 1 tablespoon hummus mixture on one side of each bread slice. Layer half of bread slices with lettuce, tomatoes, cucumber, onion, peppadew peppers and feta; top with remaining bread slices. Cut sandwiches in half.

fried green tomato parmesan

MAKES 4 SERVINGS

2 cans (15 ounces each) tomato sauce

4 green tomatoes, thickly sliced into 3 slices each

½ teaspoon salt, divided

Black pepper

½ cup all-purpose flour

1 teaspoon Italian seasoning

2 eggs

2 tablespoons water

1½ cups panko

4 tablespoons olive oil

½ cup shredded Parmesan cheese

Shredded fresh basil

Hot cooked spaghetti

1. Preheat oven to 350°F. Spread 1 cup tomato sauce in 9-inch square baking dish. Sprinkle one side of tomatoes with ¼ teaspoon salt; season lightly with pepper.

2. Combine flour, Italian seasoning and remaining ¼ teaspoon salt in shallow bowl. Whisk eggs and water in another shallow bowl. Place panko in third shallow bowl. Coat tomatoes with flour mixture. Dip in egg mixture. Dredge in panko, pressing onto all sides.

3. Heat 2 tablespoons oil in large nonstick skillet over medium-high heat. Add half of tomatoes. Cook 3 minutes per side or until panko is golden brown. Arrange tomatoes in single layer in sauce in baking dish. Sprinkle 1 teaspoon cheese on each tomato; spread some of sauce over tomatoes. Heat remaining 2 tablespoons oil in same skillet; cook remaining tomatoes 3 minutes per side until coating is golden brown. Stagger tomatoes in second layer over tomatoes in pan. Top each tomato with 1 teaspoon cheese and spread 1 cup sauce over top. Sprinkle with remaining cheese.

4. Bake 20 minutes or until cheese is melted and sauce is heated through. Heat remaining tomato sauce. Serve tomatoes with basil, spaghetti and sauce.

jap chae (korean glass noodle stir-fry)

MAKES 6 SERVINGS

5 ounces cellophane noodles (bean threads)

¼ cup soy sauce

1½ tablespoons dark sesame oil

2 teaspoons sugar

3 cloves garlic, minced

2 tablespoons vegetable oil

1 sweet potato (about 12 ounces), peeled and julienned

1 small red onion, halved and thinly sliced

1 small red bell pepper, julienned

1 large carrot, julienned

1 cup fresh shiitake mushrooms, stemmed and sliced

3 green onions, sliced

1 tablespoon sesame seeds, toasted

1. Soak noodles in hot water according to package directions. Whisk soy sauce, sesame oil, sugar and garlic in small bowl.

2. Heat vegetable oil in large skillet over high heat. Add sweet potato; cook and stir 3 minutes. Add bell pepper, onion, carrot and mushrooms; cook and stir 5 minutes or until vegetables are tender. Drain noodles; add to skillet with soy sauce mixture. Cook 2 minutes or until sauce is absorbed. Stir in green onions and sesame seeds. Serve warm, cold or at room temperature.

NOTE: This classic Korean dish is typically made with sweet potato noodles (dangmyeon). In this version, chewy cellophane noodles are mixed with ribbons of fresh sweet potato. Leftover noodles make great lunches because they're good served cold, and their flavor gets even better with more time to blend.

TIP: This is a great recipe to use your spiralizer if you have one. Use the thin ribbon blade to spiral the sweet potato, carrot, onion and bell pepper. Cut the vegetables into desired lengths.

curried quinoa burgers

MAKES 6 SERVINGS

½ cup uncooked quinoa

½ cup uncooked red lentils

1½ cups water

3 tablespoons olive oil, divided

1 medium onion, diced

1 teaspoon salt

½ cup frozen peas

3 cloves garlic, minced

2 teaspoons curry powder

1 egg

6 hamburger buns

Toppings: lettuce, sliced tomatoes, thinly sliced red onion and/or mango chutney

1. Place quinoa and lentils in fine-mesh strainer; rinse under cold water. Combine quinoa, lentils and 1½ cups water in large saucepan; bring to a boil over medium-high heat. Reduce heat to low; cover and cook 15 minutes or until quinoa is cooked and lentils are tender. Transfer to large bowl.

2. Heat 1 tablespoon oil in large nonstick skillet over medium-high heat. Add onion and salt; cook and stir 6 minutes or until onion begins to soften. Reduce heat to medium. Add peas; cook and stir 4 minutes. Add garlic and curry powder; cook 30 seconds. Add to quinoa mixture with egg; stir until combined. Cool mixture 15 minutes. Wipe out skillet.

3. Shape ½ cupfuls of mixture into ½-inch-thick patties.

4. Heat 1 tablespoon oil in same skillet over medium-high heat. Reduce heat to medium; gently place patties in skillet. Cook 4 to 5 minutes or until well browned on bottom. Add remaining 1 tablespoon oil to skillet; flip patties and cook 4 to 5 minutes or until browned on other side.

5. Serve patties on buns with desired toppings.

sweet potato and black bean tacos

MAKES 4 SERVINGS

¼ **cup sour cream**

2 **tablespoons mayonnaise**

   Juice of 1 lime

½ **teaspoon chipotle chili powder**

1 **can (about 15 ounces) black beans, undrained**

1 **teaspoon smoked paprika**

1 **sweet potato, peeled**

1 **red onion**

1 **green bell pepper**

4 **teaspoons vegetable oil, divided**

¼ **teaspoon salt**

1 **avocado, sliced**

¼ **cup chopped fresh cilantro**

¼ **cup grated cotija cheese**

8 **to 16 small taco-size tortillas**

1. Combine sour cream, mayonnaise, lime juice and chili powder in small bowl; mix well. Refrigerate until ready to use.

2. Combine beans with liquid and paprika in small saucepan. Cook over medium-low heat 5 to 7 minutes or until heated through, stirring occasionally. Remove from heat; coarsely mash beans with potato masher, leaving some beans whole. Keep warm.

3. Using a spiralizer, spiral sweet potato with medium spiral blade; cut into desired lengths. Spiral onion with fine spiral blade and bell pepper with spiral slicing blade; cut into desired lengths.

4. Heat 2 teaspoons oil in medium nonstick skillet over medium heat. Add sweet potato; cook and stir 7 to 10 minutes or until tender. Sprinkle with salt.

5. Heat remaining 2 teaspoons oil in large nonstick skillet over high heat. Add onion and bell pepper; cook and stir 5 minutes or until vegetables are browned and softened.

6. Spread beans down middle of tortillas. Top with sweet potatoes, vegetables, sour cream mixture, avocado, cilantro and cheese; fold in half.

NOTE: If you don't have a spiralizer, thinly slice the onion and bell pepper with a mandoline or sharp knife. Cut the sweet potato into julienne strips or small cubes.

pumpkin risotto

MAKES 4 SERVINGS

4 cups (32 ounces) vegetable broth

5 whole fresh sage leaves

¼ teaspoon ground nutmeg

2 tablespoons butter

1 tablespoon olive oil

1 onion, finely chopped

2 cloves garlic, minced

1½ cups uncooked arborio rice

½ cup dry white wine

1 teaspoon salt

 Black pepper

1 can (15 ounces) solid-pack pumpkin

½ cup shredded Parmesan cheese

2 tablespoons chopped fresh sage, divided

¼ cup roasted pumpkin seeds (pepitas) or chopped toasted walnuts or pecans

1. Combine broth, whole sage leaves and nutmeg in small saucepan; bring to a boil over high heat. Reduce heat to maintain a simmer.

2. Heat butter and oil in large saucepan over medium-high heat. Add onion; cook and stir 5 minutes or until softened. Add garlic; cook and stir 30 seconds. Add rice; cook 2 to 3 minutes or until rice is translucent, stirring frequently to coat with butter. Add wine, salt and pepper; cook until most of liquid is absorbed.

3. Add broth mixture, ½ cup at a time, stirring frequently until broth is absorbed before adding next ½ cup (discard whole sage leaves). Stir in pumpkin when about 1 cup broth remains. Add remaining broth; cook until rice is al dente, stirring constantly.

4. Remove from heat; stir in Parmesan and 1 tablespoon chopped sage. Cover and let stand 5 minutes. Top each serving with 1 tablespoon pumpkin seeds and remaining chopped sage.

thai veggie curry

MAKES 4 TO 6 SERVINGS

2 tablespoons vegetable oil

1 onion, quartered and thinly sliced

1 tablespoon Thai red curry paste (or to taste)

1 can (about 14 ounces) unsweetened coconut milk

2 red or yellow bell peppers, cut into strips

1½ cups cauliflower and/or broccoli florets

1 cup snow peas

1 package (about 14 ounces) tofu, pressed* and cubed

Salt and black pepper

¼ cup slivered fresh basil

Hot cooked jasmine rice

Cut tofu in half horizontally and place in between layers of paper towels. Place a weighted cutting board on top; let stand 15 to 30 minutes.

1. Heat oil in large skillet or wok over medium-high heat. Add onion; cook and stir 2 minutes or until softened. Add curry paste; cook and stir to coat onion. Add coconut milk; bring to a boil, stirring to dissolve curry paste.

2. Add bell peppers and cauliflower; simmer over medium heat 4 to 5 minutes or until crisp-tender. Stir in snow peas; simmer 2 minutes. Gently stir in tofu; cook until heated through. Season with salt and pepper.

3. Sprinkle with basil; serve with rice.

nut roast

MAKES 6 TO 8 SERVINGS

1½ cups unsalted walnuts, pecans, almonds or cashews

2 tablespoons olive oil

1 onion, finely chopped

4 ounces cremini mushrooms (about 6 large), sliced

2 cloves garlic, minced

1 can (about 14 ounces) diced tomatoes

1 cup old-fashioned oats

2 eggs, lightly beaten

2 tablespoons all-purpose flour

1 tablespoon chopped fresh sage

1 tablespoon chopped fresh parsley

1 teaspoon chopped fresh thyme

Salt and black pepper

1. Preheat oven to 350°F. Spray 8×4-inch loaf pan or baking dish with nonstick cooking spray. Place nuts in food processor. Pulse until finely chopped, allowing some larger pieces to remain. Transfer to large bowl.

2. Heat oil in medium skillet over medium heat. Add onion, mushrooms and garlic; cook and stir 3 minutes or until softened. Transfer mixture to bowl with nuts.

3. Stir in tomatoes, oats, eggs, flour, sage, parsley, thyme, salt and pepper until combined. Spoon mixture into prepared pan. Bake 45 to 50 minutes or until firm and browned. Cool slightly before slicing.

farro veggie burgers

MAKES 6 SERVINGS

1½ **cups water**

½ **cup uncooked pearled farro or spelt***

2 **medium potatoes, peeled and quartered**

2 to 4 **tablespoons canola oil, divided**

¾ **cup finely chopped green onions**

1 **cup grated carrots**

2 **teaspoons grated fresh ginger**

2 **tablespoons ground almonds**

¼ to ¾ **teaspoon salt**

¼ **teaspoon black pepper**

½ **cup panko bread crumbs**

6 **whole wheat hamburger buns**

Toppings: ketchup, mustard and/or lettuce

Use 2 cups water if using spelt.

1. Combine 1½ cups water and farro in medium saucepan; bring to a boil over high heat. Reduce heat to low; cook 25 to 30 minutes or until farro is tender. Drain and cool. (If using spelt, use 2 cups of water and cook until tender.)

2. Meanwhile, place potatoes in large saucepan; cover with water. Bring to a boil; reduce heat and simmer 20 minutes or until tender. Cool and mash potatoes; set aside.

3. Heat 1 tablespoon oil in medium skillet over medium-high heat. Add green onions; cook and stir 1 minute. Add carrots and ginger; cover and cook 2 to 3 minutes or until carrots are tender. Transfer to large bowl; cool completely.

4. Add mashed potatoes and farro to carrot mixture. Add almonds, salt and pepper; mix well. Shape mixture into six patties. Spread panko on medium plate; coat patties with panko.

5. Heat 1 tablespoon oil in large nonstick skillet over medium heat. Cook patties about 4 minutes per side or until golden brown, adding additional oil as needed. Serve on buns with desired toppings.

mushroom and vegetable ragoût over polenta

MAKES 6 SERVINGS

RAGOÛT

- 3 tablespoons olive oil
- 8 ounces sliced mushrooms
- 8 ounces shiitake mushrooms, stemmed and thinly sliced
- ½ cup Madeira wine
- 4 cloves garlic, minced
- 1 medium onion, chopped
- 1 can (about 15 ounces) chickpeas, rinsed and drained
- 1 can (about 28 ounces) crushed tomatoes
- 1 can (6 ounces) tomato paste
- 1 sprig fresh rosemary

POLENTA

- 2 cups whole milk
- 2 cups water
- ¼ teaspoon salt
- 1 cup uncooked instant polenta
- ½ cup grated Parmesan cheese

1. Heat oil in large saucepan over medium-high heat. Add mushrooms; cook and stir 8 to 10 minutes or until mushrooms are brown. Add Madeira; cook 1 minute or until liquid is reduced by one half.

2. Stir in garlic, onion, chickpeas, crushed tomatoes, tomato paste and rosemary. Cover and cook over medium-low heat about 1 hour or until vegetables are tender. Remove and discard rosemary.

3. For polenta, bring milk, water and salt to a boil in large saucepan over medium-high heat. Slowly whisk in polenta in thin steady stream. Cook 4 to 5 minutes or until thick and creamy, whisking frequently.

4. Remove polenta from heat and stir in Parmesan cheese. Top polenta with ragoût.

roasted beet risotto

MAKES 4 SERVINGS

2 medium beets, trimmed

4 cups vegetable broth

2 tablespoons butter

1 leek, finely chopped

1 cup uncooked arborio rice

1 teaspoon salt

½ cup dry white wine

½ cup crumbled goat cheese,
plus additional for garnish

1 teaspoon Italian seasoning

Juice of 1 lemon

Lemon wedges (optional)

1. Preheat oven to 400°F. Wrap each beet tightly in foil. Place on baking sheet. Roast 45 minutes to 1 hour or until knife inserted into centers goes in easily. Unwrap beets; discard foil. Let stand 15 minutes or until cool enough to handle. Peel and cut beets into bite-size pieces. Set aside.

2. Bring broth to a simmer in medium saucepan; keep warm.

3. Melt butter in large saucepan over medium-high heat. Add leek; cook and stir about 2 minutes or until softened. Add rice and ½ teaspoon salt; cook about 3 minutes or until rice is translucent around edges, stirring frequently. Add wine; cook and stir until wine is absorbed.

4. Add broth, ½ cup at a time, stirring frequently until broth is absorbed before adding next ½ cup. Continue adding broth and stirring until rice is tender and mixture is creamy, about 20 to 25 minutes. Remove from heat.

5. Stir ½ cup cheese, Italian seasoning and remaining ½ teaspoon salt into risotto. Gently stir in beets. Sprinkle with lemon juice and additional cheese, if desired. Garnish with lemon wedges.

grilled portobello and spring green sandwiches

MAKES 4 SANDWICHES

- 5 tablespoons olive oil, divided
- 1½ tablespoons balsamic vinegar
- 1 tablespoon coarse grain Dijon mustard
- 1 tablespoon water
- 1 teaspoon dried oregano
- 1 clove garlic, minced
- ½ teaspoon black pepper
- ¼ teaspoon salt
- 4 large portobello mushroom caps, wiped with damp towel, gills and stems removed
- 8 slices multigrain Italian bread
- ¼ cup crumbled blue cheese
- 2 cups spring greens

1. Combine 2 tablespoons oil, vinegar, mustard, water, oregano, garlic, pepper and salt in medium bowl. Place mushrooms on sheet of foil or large plate. Brush 2 tablespoons dressing over mushrooms; reserve remaining dressing. Let mushrooms stand 30 minutes.

2. Brush grill pan with 1 tablespoon oil; heat over medium-high heat. Brush both sides of bread slices with remaining 2 tablespoons oil. Grill bread 1 minute per side, pressing down with spatula to flatten slightly. Set aside.

3. Grill mushrooms 3 to 4 minutes per side or until tender. Place each mushroom on one bread slice. Sprinkle with blue cheese.

4. Combine spring greens and reserved dressing. Arrange spring greens on top of mushrooms; top with remaining bread slices.

black bean burgers with spicy mayo

MAKES 4 SERVINGS

5 whole wheat hamburger buns (1½ to 2 ounces each), split, divided

1 can (about 15 ounces) black beans, rinsed and drained

½ cup (2 ounces) shredded Cheddar cheese or Mexican blend cheese

2 egg whites

2 green onions, sliced

1 teaspoon chili powder

1 teaspoon dried oregano

½ teaspoon garlic salt

1 tablespoon canola oil

2 tablespoons mayonnaise

¾ teaspoon chipotle hot pepper sauce

4 lettuce leaves

4 large thin tomato slices

1. Tear one hamburger bun into pieces; place in bowl of food processor. Process until coarse crumbs form. Place in medium bowl.

2. Place black beans, cheese, egg whites, green onions, chili powder, oregano and garlic salt in food processor. Process until thick paste forms, scraping side of bowl once. Add mixture to bread crumbs in bowl; mix well.

3. Heat oil in large nonstick skillet over medium heat. Drop mixture by ½ cupfuls into skillet; press down to form 4-inch patties. Cook 4 minutes per side or until browned. Lightly toast remaining hamburger buns, if desired.

4. Combine mayonnaise and hot pepper sauce in small bowl. Serve patties in buns with chipotle mayonnaise, lettuce and tomato.

SIDES & SNACKS

artichoke pesto with lavash chips

MAKES ABOUT 1½ CUPS

3 pieces lavash bread (about 7×9 inches)

¼ cup plus 2 tablespoons olive oil, divided

¾ teaspoon coarse salt, divided

1 can (14 ounces) artichoke hearts, rinsed and drained

½ cup chopped walnuts, toasted*

¼ cup packed fresh basil leaves

2 tablespoons lemon juice

1 clove garlic, minced

¼ cup grated Parmesan cheese

*To toast walnuts, spread on baking sheet. Bake in preheated 350°F oven 6 to 8 minutes or until golden brown, stirring once or twice.

1. Preheat oven to 350°F. Line baking sheet with parchment paper.

2. Brush both sides of each piece lavash with 2 tablespoons oil. Sprinkle with ¼ teaspoon salt. Place on prepared baking sheet. Bake 10 minutes or until lavash is crisp and browned. Cool completely on wire rack.

3. Place artichoke hearts, walnuts, basil, lemon juice, garlic and remaining ½ teaspoon salt in food processor; pulse until coarsely chopped. With motor running, add remaining ¼ cup oil in thin steady stream; process until smooth. Add cheese; pulse until blended.

4. Break lavash into chips. Serve with pesto.

rosemary-lemon pork kabobs

MAKES 4 SERVINGS

4 small red potatoes, quartered

1 pork tenderloin (about 1 pound), cut into 16 (1-inch) cubes

1 small red onion, quartered and layers separated

2 tablespoons extra virgin olive oil

½ teaspoon dried rosemary
   Dash paprika

2 tablespoons lemon juice

1 teaspoon grated lemon peel

½ clove garlic, minced

½ teaspoon salt

⅛ teaspoon black pepper

1. Preheat broiler.

2. Place steamer basket in medium saucepan; fill with water not touching bottom of basket. Bring to a boil over high heat. Add potatoes; cover and steam potatoes 6 minutes or until crisp-tender. Rinse under cold water; dry with paper towels.

3. Thread potatoes onto 4 (10-inch) metal skewers, alternating with pork and onion. Brush with 1 tablespoon oil; sprinkle with rosemary and paprika.

4. Place kabobs on baking sheet; broil 4 minutes. Turn over; broil 4 minutes more or until pork is barely pink in center.

5. Meanwhile, whisk lemon juice, lemon peel, remaining 1 tablespoon oil, garlic, salt and pepper in small bowl. Serve with kabobs.

TIP: For an artful presentation, serve the pork, potatoes and onion on rosemary sprigs. Broil the skewers as directed, then remove the food and thread it onto short rosemary sprigs.

toasted peanut couscous salad

MAKES 4 SERVINGS

½ cup water

¼ cup uncooked couscous

½ cup finely chopped red onion

½ cup finely chopped green bell pepper

1 ounce dry-roasted peanuts

1 tablespoon soy sauce

2 teaspoons cider vinegar

1½ teaspoons dark sesame oil

½ teaspoon grated fresh ginger

½ teaspoon sugar

¼ teaspoon salt

⅛ teaspoon red pepper flakes

1. Bring water to a boil in small saucepan over high heat. Remove from heat; stir in couscous. Cover tightly and let stand 5 minutes or until water is absorbed. Place in medium bowl; cool slightly. Stir in onion and bell pepper.

2. Heat small nonstick skillet over medium-high heat until hot. Add peanuts; cook 2 to 3 minutes or until beginning to turn golden, stirring frequently. Add to couscous.

3. Whisk soy sauce, vinegar, oil, ginger, sugar, salt and red pepper flakes in small bowl. Add to couscous; stir until well blended.

simple golden cornbread

MAKES 9 TO 12 SERVINGS

1¼ cups all-purpose flour

¾ cup yellow cornmeal

⅓ cup sugar

2 teaspoons baking powder

1 teaspoon salt

1¼ cups whole milk

¼ cup (½ stick) butter, melted

1 egg

Honey Butter (recipe follows, optional)

1. Preheat oven to 400°F. Spray 8-inch square baking dish or pan with nonstick cooking spray.

2. Combine flour, cornmeal, sugar, baking powder and salt in large bowl; mix well. Whisk milk, butter and egg in medium bowl until well blended. Add to flour mixture; stir just until dry ingredients are moistened. Pour batter into prepared baking dish.

3. Bake about 25 minutes or until golden brown and toothpick inserted into center comes out clean. Prepare Honey Butter, if desired. Serve with cornbread.

HONEY BUTTER: Beat 6 tablespoons (¾ stick) softened butter and ¼ cup honey in medium bowl with electric mixer at medium-high speed until light and creamy.

salsa

MAKES 4½ CUPS

1 can (28 ounces) whole Italian plum tomatoes, undrained

2 fresh plum tomatoes, seeded and coarsely chopped

2 tablespoons canned diced mild green chiles

1 tablespoon canned diced jalapeño peppers (optional)

1 tablespoon white vinegar

1 clove garlic, minced

1 teaspoon onion powder

1 teaspoon sugar

1 teaspoon ground cumin

½ teaspoon garlic powder

¼ teaspoon salt

Combine tomatoes with juice, fresh tomatoes, green chiles, jalapeños, if desired, vinegar, garlic, onion powder, sugar, cumin, garlic powder and salt in food processor; process until finely chopped.

guacamole

MAKES 2 CUPS

2 large ripe avocados

2 teaspoons fresh lime juice

¼ cup finely chopped red onion

2 tablespoons chopped fresh cilantro

½ jalapeño pepper, finely chopped

½ teaspoon salt

Corn tortilla chips, store-bought or homemade (page 166)

1. Peel and pit avocados. Place avocados in large bowl; sprinkle with lime juice and toss to coat. Mash to desired consistency with fork or potato masher.

2. Add onion, cilantro, jalapeño and salt; stir gently until well blended. Taste and add additional salt, if desired. Serve with tortilla chips.

rainbow vegetable tart

MAKES 8 TO 10 SERVINGS

1 medium red beet, peeled, halved and thinly sliced

1 medium golden beet, peeled, halved and thinly sliced

1 small butternut squash, peeled, halved and thinly sliced

2 cloves garlic, unpeeled

2 tablespoons olive oil, divided

1 teaspoon salt, divided

Black pepper

1 log (4 ounces) goat cheese, softened

2 tablespoons milk or water

2 teaspoons fresh thyme leaves

2 teaspoons honey, plus additional for drizzling

1 sheet puff pastry (half of 17-ounce package)

4 to 8 asparagus spears, ends trimmed*

If your asparagus is thick with woody stems, use a vegetable peeler to remove some of the tough bits.

1. Preheat oven to 400°F.

2. Spread beets and butternut squash on large baking sheet, keeping each vegetable separate. Place garlic on baking sheet. Drizzle 1 tablespoon oil over vegetables and sprinkle with ½ teaspoon salt and pepper. Bake 25 to 30 minutes or until vegetables are crisp-tender, turning vegetables once or twice.

3. Line another large baking sheet with parchment paper. Combine goat cheese, milk, thyme, 2 teaspoons honey and remaining ½ teaspoon salt in large bowl; season with pepper and squeeze garlic from skins into bowl. Beat with electric mixer at medium speed until well blended. Unfold pastry on prepared baking sheet; roll with rolling pin into rectangle. Spread goat cheese mixture over pastry. Arrange roasted vegetables and asparagus over cheese. Drizzle with remaining 1 tablespoon oil and lightly drizzle with additional honey.

4. Bake 15 minutes or until pastry is puffed and golden brown and vegetables are tender. Serve warm or at room temperature.

mediterranean barley-bean salad

MAKES 4 SERVINGS

⅔ cup uncooked pearl barley

3 cups asparagus pieces

2 cans (about 15 ounces each) dark red kidney beans, rinsed and drained

2 tablespoons chopped fresh mint

¼ cup lemon juice

¼ cup Italian salad dressing

¼ teaspoon black pepper

¼ cup dry-roasted sunflower seeds

1. Cook barley according to package directions. Add asparagus during last 5 minutes of cooking; drain. Transfer to large bowl; refrigerate at least 2 hours.

2. Stir beans and mint into barley mixture. Whisk lemon juice, salad dressing and pepper in small bowl until well blended. Add to barley mixture; toss to coat. Sprinkle with sunflower seeds.

quinoa and roasted corn

MAKES 6 TO 8 SERVINGS

1 cup uncooked quinoa

2 cups water

½ teaspoon salt

4 ears corn or 2 cups frozen
  corn

¼ cup plus 1 tablespoon
  vegetable oil, divided

1 cup chopped green onions,
  divided

1 teaspoon coarse salt

1 cup quartered grape tomatoes
  or chopped plum tomatoes,
  drained*

1 cup black beans, rinsed and
  drained

  Juice of 1 lime (about
  2 tablespoons)

¼ teaspoon grated lime peel

¼ teaspoon sugar

¼ teaspoon ground cumin

¼ teaspoon black pepper

  *Place tomatoes in fine-mesh strainer
  and place over bowl 10 to 15 minutes.*

1. Place quinoa in fine-mesh strainer; rinse well under cold water. Combine quinoa, 2 cups water and salt in medium saucepan; bring to a boil over high heat. Reduce heat to low; cover and simmer 15 to 18 minutes or until quinoa is tender and water is absorbed. Transfer to large bowl.

2. Meanwhile, remove husks and silk from corn; cut kernels off cobs. Heat ¼ cup oil in large skillet over medium-high heat. Add corn; cook 10 to 12 minutes or until tender and lightly browned, stirring occasionally. Stir in ⅔ cup green onions and coarse salt; cook and stir 2 minutes. Add corn mixture to quinoa. Gently stir in tomatoes and black beans.

3. Combine lime juice, lime peel, sugar, cumin and pepper in small bowl. Whisk in remaining 1 tablespoon oil until blended. Pour over quinoa mixture; toss lightly to coat. Sprinkle with remaining ⅓ cup green onions. Serve warm or chilled.

tomato and cheese focaccia

MAKES 1 (10-INCH) BREAD

1 package (¼ ounce) active dry yeast

¾ cup warm water (105° to 115°F)

2 cups all-purpose flour

½ teaspoon salt

4 tablespoons olive oil, divided

1 teaspoon Italian seasoning

8 oil-packed sun-dried tomatoes, well drained

½ cup (2 ounces) shredded provolone cheese

¼ cup grated Parmesan cheese

1. Dissolve yeast in warm water in small bowl; let stand 5 minutes. Combine flour and salt in food processor. Add yeast mixture and 3 tablespoons oil; process until ingredients form a ball. Process 1 minute.

2. Turn dough out onto lightly floured surface. Knead about 2 minutes or until smooth and elastic. Place dough in oiled bowl; turn dough over to grease top. Cover and let rise in warm place about 30 minutes or until doubled in bulk.

3. Punch down dough. Let rest 5 minutes. Press dough into oiled 10-inch round cake pan, deep-dish pizza pan or springform pan. Brush with remaining 1 tablespoon oil; sprinkle with Italian seasoning. Press sun-dried tomatoes into top of dough; sprinkle with cheeses. Cover and let rise in warm place 15 minutes.

4. Preheat oven to 425°F. Bake 20 to 25 minutes or until golden brown. Cut into wedges to serve.

NOTE: If mixing dough by hand, combine flour and salt in large bowl. Stir in yeast mixture and 3 tablespoons oil until a ball forms. Turn out onto lightly floured surface and knead about 10 minutes or until smooth and elastic. Proceed as directed.

lentil and orzo pasta salad

MAKES 4 SERVINGS

8 cups water

½ cup dried lentils, rinsed and sorted

4 ounces uncooked orzo

1½ cups quartered cherry tomatoes or halved grape tomatoes

¾ cup finely chopped celery

½ cup chopped red onion

2 ounces pitted olives (about 16 olives), coarsely chopped

3 to 4 tablespoons cider vinegar

1 tablespoon extra virgin olive oil

1 tablespoon dried basil

1 clove garlic, minced

⅛ teaspoon red pepper flakes

4 ounces feta cheese with sun-dried tomatoes and basil

1. Bring water to a boil in large saucepan over high heat. Add lentils; boil 12 minutes.

2. Add orzo; cook 10 minutes or just until tender. Drain. Rinse under cold water to cool completely. Drain well.

3. Meanwhile, combine tomatoes, celery, onion, olives, vinegar, oil, basil, garlic and pepper flakes in large bowl.

4. Add lentil mixture; toss gently to blend. Add cheese; toss gently. Let stand 15 minutes before serving.

creamy cashew spread

MAKES ABOUT ½ CUP

1 cup raw cashews

2 tablespoons lemon juice

1 tablespoon tahini

½ teaspoon salt

½ teaspoon black pepper

2 teaspoons minced fresh herbs, such as basil, parsley or oregano (optional)

Assorted bread toasts and/or crackers

1. Rinse cashews and place in medium bowl. Cover with water by at least 2 inches. Soak 4 hours or overnight. Drain cashews, reserving soaking water.

2. Place cashews, 2 tablespoons reserved water, lemon juice, tahini, salt and pepper in food processor or blender; process several minutes or until smooth. Add additional water, 1 tablespoon at a time, until desired consistency is reached.

3. Cover and refrigerate until ready to serve. Stir in herbs, if desired, just before serving. Serve with desired crackers.

TIP: Use as a spread or dip for hors d'oeuvres, or as a sandwich spread or pasta topping. Thin with additional liquid as needed.

corn tortilla chips

MAKES 6 TO 8 DOZEN CHIPS

12 (6-inch) corn tortillas,
 preferably day-old
Vegetable oil
½ to 1 teaspoon salt

1. If tortillas are fresh, let stand, uncovered, in single layer on wire rack 1 to 2 hours to dry slightly.

2. Stack 6 tortillas; cut tortillas into 6 or 8 equal wedges through stack. Repeat with remaining tortillas.

3. Heat ½ inch oil in deep heavy skillet over medium-high heat to 375°F; adjust heat to maintain temperature.

4. Fry tortilla wedges in a single layer 1 minute or until crisp, turning occasionally. Remove with slotted spoon; drain on paper towels. Repeat until all chips have been fried. Sprinkle chips with salt.

naan (indian flatbread)

MAKES 12 SERVINGS

1 packet (¼ ounce) active dry yeast

1 teaspoon sugar

¼ cup plus 2 tablespoons warm water, divided

3 cups all-purpose flour

1 teaspoon salt

1 teaspoon kalonji* seeds or poppy seeds (optional)

½ cup plain whole milk Greek yogurt

¼ cup (½ stick) butter, melted, plus additional butter for brushing on naan

Kalonji seed is often called onion seed or black cumin seed. It is available in Indian markets and is traditional in some varieties of naan.

1. Stir yeast and sugar into 2 tablespoons water in small bowl. Let stand 10 minutes or until foamy. Place flour, salt and kalonji, if desired, in bowl of stand mixer. Attach dough hook; stir until blended.

2. Add yeast mixture, yogurt and ¼ cup butter; mix on low speed until combined. Add remaining ¼ cup water by tablespoonfuls, mixing on low speed until dough comes together and cleans side of bowl. (You may not need all the water.) Knead at low speed 5 to 7 minutes or until dough is smooth and elastic.

3. Shape dough into a ball and place in greased bowl, turning to grease top. Let rise in warm place 1½ to 2 hours or until doubled.

4. Punch dough down; divide into 6 pieces. Roll into balls and place on plate sprayed with nonstick cooking spray. Cover and let rest 10 to 15 minutes.

5. Meanwhile, prepare grill for direct cooking or preheat oven to 500°F with baking stone on rack in lower third of oven. (Remove other racks.) Place each ball of dough on lightly floured surface; roll and stretch into ⅛-inch-thick oval.

6. Place on grill or baking stone 2 or 3 at a time. Grill, covered, or bake 2 minutes until puffed. Turn, brush tops with additional butter and grill or bake 1 to 2 minutes until browned in patches on both sides. Brush bottom with butter; serve warm.

farmers' market potato salad

MAKES 6 SERVINGS

Pickled Red Onions (recipe follows)

2 cups cubed assorted potatoes (purple, baby red, Yukon Gold and/or a combination)

1 cup green beans, cut into 1-inch pieces

2 tablespoons plain Greek yogurt

2 tablespoons white wine vinegar

2 tablespoons olive oil

1 tablespoon spicy mustard

1 teaspoon salt

1. Prepare pickled red onions.

2. Bring large saucepan of water to a boil. Add potatoes; cook 5 to 8 minutes or until fork-tender. Add green beans during last 4 minutes of cooking time. Drain potatoes and green beans.

3. Stir yogurt, vinegar, oil, mustard and salt in large bowl until smooth and well blended.

4. Add potatoes, green beans and onions to dressing; gently toss to coat. Cover and refrigerate at least 1 hour to allow flavors to develop before serving.

pickled red onions

MAKES ABOUT ½ CUP

2 tablespoons water

1 teaspoon sugar

½ teaspoon salt

½ cup thinly sliced red onion

¼ cup white wine vinegar

Heat water, sugar and salt in small saucepan until sugar is dissolved. Pour into large glass jar. Add onion and vinegar. Seal jar; shake well. Refrigerate at least 1 hour or up to 1 week.

DESSERTS

fruit tart

MAKES 8 TO 10 SERVINGS

CRUST
- 2 whole wheat naan (6 ounces total), torn into large pieces
- 3 tablespoons sugar
- ¼ cup (½ stick) butter, melted

FILLING
- 8 ounces cream cheese, cut into 1-inch cubes, softened
- 3 tablespoons sugar
- 1 tablespoon lemon juice
- 1 teaspoon vanilla

TOPPING
- 2 kiwi, peeled and sliced
- Assorted fresh berries
- 2 tablespoons apricot jam, warmed

1. Preheat oven to 350°F. Line baking sheet with parchment paper; place 9-inch round fluted tart pan on prepared baking sheet.

2. Place naan pieces in food processor. Process until fine crumbs form, yielding about 2 cups. Add sugar; pulse to blend. Add butter; pulse until combined.

3. Press crumbs firmly in bottom and up sides of tart pan. Bake 25 to 30 minutes until crust is set and golden brown. Place on wire rack; cool completely.

4. Beat cream cheese, sugar, lemon juice and vanilla with electric mixer on medium speed 30 seconds. Pour filling into cooled tart shell; smooth evenly with spatula.

5. Arrange kiwi and berries on top of tart. Brush fruit with warmed jam. Refrigerate 20 minutes before serving.

mixed berry crisp

MAKES ABOUT 9 SERVINGS

6 cups mixed berries, thawed if frozen

¾ cup packed brown sugar, divided

¼ cup quick-cooking tapioca

Juice of ½ lemon

1 teaspoon ground cinnamon

½ cup rice flour or all-purpose flour

6 tablespoons (¾ stick) cold butter, cut into small pieces

½ cup sliced almonds

1. Preheat oven to 375°F. Spray 8- or 9-inch square baking dish with nonstick cooking spray.

2. Combine berries, ¼ cup brown sugar, tapioca, lemon juice and cinnamon in large bowl; toss to coat. Spoon into prepared baking dish.

3. Combine rice flour, remaining ½ cup brown sugar and butter in food processor; pulse until mixture resembles coarse crumbs. Add almonds; pulse until combined. (Leave some large pieces of almonds.) Sprinkle over berry mixture.

4. Bake 20 to 30 minutes or topping is until golden brown.

warm apple crostata

MAKES 4 TARTS (4 TO 8 SERVINGS)

1¾ cups all-purpose flour

⅓ cup granulated sugar

½ teaspoon plus ⅛ teaspoon salt, divided

¾ cup (1½ sticks) cold butter, cut into pieces

3 tablespoons ice water

2 teaspoons vanilla

8 Pink Lady or Honeycrisp apples (about 1½ pounds), peeled and cut into ¼-inch slices

¼ cup packed brown sugar

1 tablespoon lemon juice

1 teaspoon ground cinnamon

⅛ teaspoon ground nutmeg

4 teaspoons butter, cut into very small pieces

1 egg, beaten

1 to 2 teaspoons coarse sugar

Vanilla ice cream

Caramel sauce or ice cream topping

1. Combine flour, ⅓ cup granulated sugar and ½ teaspoon salt in food processor; process 5 seconds. Add ¾ cup butter; process about 10 seconds or until mixture resembles coarse crumbs.

2. Combine ice water and vanilla in small bowl. With motor running, pour mixture through feed tube; process 12 seconds or until dough begins to come together. Shape dough into a disc; wrap in plastic wrap and refrigerate 30 minutes.

3. Meanwhile, combine apples, brown sugar, lemon juice, cinnamon, nutmeg and remaining ⅛ teaspoon salt in large bowl; toss to coat. Preheat oven to 400°F.

4. Line two baking sheets with parchment paper. Cut dough into 4 pieces; roll out each piece into 7-inch circle on floured surface. Place circles on prepared baking sheets; mound apples in center of dough circles (about 1 cup apples for each crostata). Fold or roll up edges of dough towards center to create rim of crostata. Dot apples with 4 teaspoons butter. Brush dough with egg; sprinkle dough and apples with coarse sugar.

5. Bake about 20 minutes or until apples are tender and crust is golden brown. Serve warm topped with ice cream and caramel sauce.

cherry-almond clafoutis

MAKES 4 SERVINGS

½ cup slivered almonds, toasted*

½ cup powdered sugar

⅔ cup all-purpose flour

⅔ cup granulated sugar

¼ teaspoon salt

½ cup (1 stick) cold butter, cut into pieces

⅔ cup milk

2 eggs

½ teaspoon vanilla

1 cup fresh cherries, pitted and quartered or 1 cup raspberries

To toast almonds, spread in single layer on baking sheet. Bake in preheated 350°F oven 8 to 10 minutes or until golden brown, stirring once or twice.

1. Preheat oven to 350°F. Spray four (6-ounce) ramekins with nonstick cooking spray; place on baking sheet.

2. Process almonds in food processor until coarsely ground. Add powdered sugar; pulse until well blended. Add flour, granulated sugar and salt. Pulse until well blended. Gradually add butter through feed tube, pulsing just until blended.

3. Combine milk, eggs and vanilla in small bowl. With motor running, gradually add milk mixture to almond mixture. Process until blended. Remove blade from food processor; gently stir in cherries.

4. Divide batter among prepared ramekins. Bake about 50 minutes or until tops and sides are puffy and golden. Let cool 5 to 10 minutes.

NOTE: Clafoutis is a traditional French dessert made by layering a sweet batter over fresh fruit. The result is a rich dessert with a cake-like topping and a pudding-like center.

pineapple upside down cake

MAKES 10 SERVINGS

TOPPING

- 1 small pineapple
- ¼ cup (½ stick) butter
- ½ cup packed brown sugar
  Maraschino cherries

CAKE

- 2 cups all-purpose flour
- 2 teaspoons baking powder
- ½ teaspoon baking soda
- ½ teaspoon salt
- ½ cup (1 stick) butter, softened
- 1 cup granulated sugar
- 1 egg
- 1 teaspoon vanilla
- 1 cup buttermilk

1. Preheat oven to 350°F. Spray 9-inch round baking pan with nonstick cooking spray. Remove top and bottom of pineapple. Cut off outside of pineapple and remove eyes. Cut pineapple crosswise into ¼-inch slices. Remove core with ½-inch cookie cutter or sharp knife.

2. For topping, cook and stir ¼ cup butter and brown sugar in medium skillet over medium heat until melted and smooth. Remove from heat. Pour into prepared pan. Arrange pineapple slices in pan, placing cherries in centers of pineapple and between slices. Reserve remaining pineapple for another use.

3. Combine flour, baking powder, baking soda and salt in medium bowl. Beat ½ cup butter and granulated sugar in large bowl with electric mixer on medium speed until well blended. Beat in egg and vanilla. Add flour mixture alternately with buttermilk, mixing on low speed just until blended after each addition. Pour batter over pineapple.

4. Bake about 1 hour or until toothpick inserted into center comes out clean. Cool in pan on wire rack 10 minutes. Run thin knife around edge of pan to loosen cake. Invert onto serving plate. Cool completely.

NOTE: The cake can also be baked in a 12-inch cast iron skillet. Melt the butter and sugar in the skillet, add the pineapple and cherries and pour the batter over the fruit. Check the cake for doneness at 40 minutes.

berry-peach cobbler

MAKES 8 SERVINGS

4 tablespoons plus 2 teaspoons sugar, divided

¾ cup plus 2 tablespoons all-purpose flour, divided

1¼ pounds peaches, peeled and sliced *or* 1 package (16 ounces) frozen unsweetened sliced peaches, thawed and drained

2 cups fresh raspberries *or* 1 package (12 ounces) frozen unsweetened raspberries

1 teaspoon grated lemon peel

½ teaspoon baking powder

½ teaspoon baking soda

⅛ teaspoon salt

2 tablespoons cold butter, cut into small pieces

¼ cup plus 1 tablespoon buttermilk

¼ cup plain Greek yogurt

1. Preheat oven to 425°F. Spray eight ramekins or 11×7-inch baking dish with nonstick cooking spray; place ramekins in jelly-roll pan.

2. Combine 2 tablespoons sugar and 2 tablespoons flour in large bowl. Add peaches, raspberries and lemon peel; toss to coat. Divide fruit evenly among prepared ramekins. Bake 15 minutes or until fruit is bubbly around edges.

3. Meanwhile, combine 2 tablespoons sugar, remaining ¾ cup flour, baking powder, baking soda and salt in medium bowl. Cut in butter with pastry blender or fingers until mixture resembles coarse crumbs. Stir in buttermilk and yogurt just until dry ingredients are moistened.

4. Remove ramekins from oven; top fruit with equal dollops of topping. Sprinkle topping with remaining 2 teaspoons sugar. Bake 18 to 20 minutes or until topping is lightly browned. Serve warm.

swedish apple pie

MAKES 1 (9-INCH) PIE

4 Granny Smith apples, peeled, cored and sliced

1 cup plus 1 tablespoon sugar, divided

1 tablespoon ground cinnamon

¾ cup (1½ sticks) butter, melted

1 cup all-purpose flour

½ cup chopped nuts

2 eggs

½ teaspoon salt

1. Preheat oven to 350°F.

2. Spread apples in 9-inch deep-dish pie plate or 9-inch square baking dish. Combine 1 tablespoon sugar and cinnamon in small bowl; sprinkle over apples and drizzle with butter.

3. Combine remaining 1 cup sugar, flour, nuts, eggs and salt in medium bowl. (Mixture will be thick.) Spread batter over apples.

4. Bake 50 to 55 minutes or until top is golden brown.

cardamom shortbread

MAKES 16 LARGE COOKIES

2 cups all-purpose flour

1 teaspoon ground cardamom

½ teaspoon baking powder

½ teaspoon salt

¾ cup (1½ sticks) butter, softened

¼ cup powdered sugar

3 tablespoons honey

3 teaspoons granulated sugar

1. Preheat oven to 300°F.

2. Combine flour, cardamom, baking powder and salt in medium bowl; set aside. Beat butter, powdered sugar and honey in large bowl with electric mixer on medium speed until light and creamy. Add flour mixture; beat until mixture resembles coarse crumbs.

3. Transfer dough to lightly floured surface. Knead 10 times; divide in half. Working with one half at a time, shape dough into a ball.

4. Place ball between two sheets of parchment paper; roll into 8-inch circle. Remove top piece of parchment; place dough on ungreased cookie sheet. Trim dough to make circle (place 8-inch plate or bowl on dough and trim around edge). Score dough into eight wedges. Sprinkle evenly with granulated sugar.

5. Bake 20 to 25 minutes or until golden brown. Remove shortbread and parchment to wire racks; cool 10 minutes. Transfer to cutting board; cut along score lines. Store in airtight container for up to 10 days or freeze for longer storage.

apple blackberry crisp

MAKES 6 SERVINGS

4 cups sliced peeled apples
 Juice of ½ lemon

2 tablespoons granulated sugar

2 tablespoons Irish cream
  liqueur

1 teaspoon ground cinnamon,
  divided

1 cup old-fashioned oats

6 tablespoons (¾ stick) cold
  butter, cut into small pieces

⅔ cup packed brown sugar

¼ cup all-purpose flour

1 cup fresh blackberries
 Irish Whipped Cream (recipe
  follows, optional)

1. Preheat oven to 375°F. Grease 9-inch oval or 8-inch square baking dish.

2. Place apples in large bowl; drizzle with lemon juice. Add granulated sugar, liqueur and ½ teaspoon cinnamon; toss to coat.

3. Combine oats, butter, brown sugar, flour and remaining ½ teaspoon cinnamon in food processor; pulse until combined, leaving some large pieces.

4. Gently stir blackberries into apple mixture. Spoon into prepared baking dish; sprinkle with oat mixture.

5. Bake 30 to 40 minutes or until filling is bubbly and topping is golden brown. Prepare Irish Whipped Cream, if desired; serve with crisp.

IRISH WHIPPED CREAM: Beat 1 cup whipping cream and 2 tablespoons Irish cream liqueur in large bowl with electric mixer at high speed until slightly thickened. Add 1 to 2 tablespoons powdered sugar; beat until soft peaks form.

TIP: This crisp can also be made without the blackberries; just add an additional 1 cup sliced apples.

berry crisp with brown sugar-almond topping

MAKES 8 SERVINGS

2 cups fresh or thawed frozen blackberries, undrained

2 cups fresh or thawed frozen raspberries, undrained

1 cup fresh or thawed frozen blueberries, undrained

½ cup plus 3 tablespoons all-purpose flour, divided

½ cup sugar

1½ teaspoons grated fresh ginger

1 teaspoon vanilla

½ cup old-fashioned oats

¼ teaspoon ground cinnamon

¼ teaspoon salt

¼ cup (½ stick) butter, cut into small pieces

¼ cup slivered almonds

3 tablespoons packed dark brown sugar

1. Preheat oven to 350°F. Spray 9-inch square baking dish with nonstick cooking spray.

2. Combine blackberries, raspberries, blueberries with liquid, 3 tablespoons flour, sugar, ginger and vanilla in large bowl; mix well. Spoon into prepared baking dish.

3. Combine remaining ½ cup flour, oats, cinnamon and salt in medium bowl. Cut in butter with pastry blender or fingers until mixture resembles coarse crumbs. Spoon evenly over berry mixture. Sprinkle with almonds, then brown sugar.

4. Bake 30 minutes or until filling is bubbly. Cool on wire rack 30 minutes.

metric conversion chart

VOLUME MEASUREMENTS (dry)

$1/8$ teaspoon = 0.5 mL
$1/4$ teaspoon = 1 mL
$1/2$ teaspoon = 2 mL
$3/4$ teaspoon = 4 mL
1 teaspoon = 5 mL
1 tablespoon = 15 mL
2 tablespoons = 30 mL
$1/4$ cup = 60 mL
$1/3$ cup = 75 mL
$1/2$ cup = 125 mL
$2/3$ cup = 150 mL
$3/4$ cup = 175 mL
1 cup = 250 mL
2 cups = 1 pint = 500 mL
3 cups = 750 mL
4 cups = 1 quart = 1 L

VOLUME MEASUREMENTS (fluid)

1 fluid ounce (2 tablespoons) = 30 mL
4 fluid ounces ($1/2$ cup) = 125 mL
8 fluid ounces (1 cup) = 250 mL
12 fluid ounces ($1 1/2$ cups) = 375 mL
16 fluid ounces (2 cups) = 500 mL

WEIGHTS (mass)

$1/2$ ounce = 15 g
1 ounce = 30 g
3 ounces = 90 g
4 ounces = 120 g
8 ounces = 225 g
10 ounces = 285 g
12 ounces = 360 g
16 ounces = 1 pound = 450 g

DIMENSIONS

$1/16$ inch = 2 mm
$1/8$ inch = 3 mm
$1/4$ inch = 6 mm
$1/2$ inch = 1.5 cm
$3/4$ inch = 2 cm
1 inch = 2.5 cm

OVEN TEMPERATURES

250°F = 120°C
275°F = 140°C
300°F = 150°C
325°F = 160°C
350°F = 180°C
375°F = 190°C
400°F = 200°C
425°F = 220°C
450°F = 230°C

BAKING PAN SIZES

Utensil	Size in Inches/Quarts	Metric Volume	Size in Centimeters
Baking or Cake Pan (square or rectangular)	8×8×2	2 L	20×20×5
	9×9×2	2.5 L	23×23×5
	12×8×2	3 L	30×20×5
	13×9×2	3.5 L	33×23×5
Loaf Pan	8×4×3	1.5 L	20×10×7
	9×5×3	2 L	23×13×7
Round Layer Cake Pan	8×1½	1.2 L	20×4
	9×1½	1.5 L	23×4
Pie Plate	8×1¼	750 mL	20×3
	9×1¼	1 L	23×3
Baking Dish or Casserole	1 quart	1 L	—
	1½ quart	1.5 L	—
	2 quart	2 L	—